The Bald Bandit
光头劫匪

[美] 罗恩·罗伊 著
[美] 约翰·史蒂文·格尼 绘　曹幼南 译

人物介绍

丁丁

三人小组的成员，聪明勇敢，喜欢读推理小说，紧急关头总能保持头脑冷静。喜欢在做事之前好好思考！

三人小组的成员，活泼机智，喜欢吃好吃的食物，常常有意想不到的点子。

乔希

露丝

三人小组的成员，活泼开朗，喜欢从头到脚穿同一种颜色的衣服，总是那个能找到大部分线索的人。

幸运儿奥利里

长着红头发的瘦高个高中生，在绿地储蓄银行门口用像机拍到了劫匪的正脸。

自称是绿地储蓄银行雇用的私家侦探，受雇调查银行抢劫案。

雷迪侦探

霍华德先生

霍华德理发店的老板，帮助丁丁清洗了染上鞋油的头发。

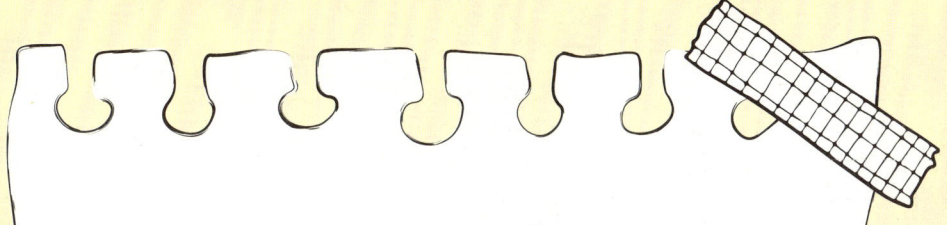

字母 B 代表 big bucks,一大笔钱……

侦探看着三个孩子。

"我有个提议。"他开口道,"你们明天去高中查一查。如果你们找到那个拍摄到劫匪的男孩,拿到录像带,然后交给我,你们可以得到一笔相当丰厚的奖金。"

"多少钱?"乔希问。

"每人一百美元怎么样?"

"一百美元?"露丝激动得尖声叫了出来。

…………

侦探掏出便笺簿和铅笔,在一张纸上写了一行数字,然后将纸撕了下来。

"这是我的电话号码,拿到录像带后就给我打电话。"

雷迪侦探走后,丁丁关上门。他笑得合不拢嘴,对乔希和露丝说:"每人一百美元!我们要发财了!"

第一章

丁丁将塑料尖牙塞进嘴里,朝着他最好的朋友乔希·平托做了一个吓人的鬼脸。

"我像个吸血鬼吗?"这样说话很难不喷出口水来,于是丁丁又把尖牙取了出来。

丁丁的全名是唐纳德·戴维·邓肯,但只有他妈妈在生气的时候才叫他唐纳德,而且是连名带姓一起叫。

乔希咧嘴笑道:"不像。你就像一个骨瘦如柴,戴着假牙的三年级学生。"

"等我穿上服装你再看。"丁丁说,"到时我就像吸血鬼了。"

"可能会像,"乔希正把一块绿色的床单撕成长布条,"也可能不像。"

丁丁的宠物豚鼠洛蕾塔在绿布条里爬来爬去,时不时发出好奇的吱吱声。

"你要是用那些布条把自己包裹起来,该怎么走路?"丁丁问乔希。

乔希继续撕着床单。"沼泽里的怪物不是靠走的,"他故意拖长声音,有种滑溜溜的感觉,"而是靠滑——行。"

"好吧,你裹着这些布条,怎么滑——行呢?"

这时,门铃响了。丁丁打开门,站在台阶上的是住在隔壁的邻居露丝。

"嘿!露丝,你怎么戴着假发?明天才是万圣夜。"

露丝穿着她平常穿的亮丽衣服——粉色的衬衣、粉色的裤子、粉色的运动鞋。但是,她头上

戴着一顶乌黑发亮的假发,脸上还粘着浓密的假眉毛。

露丝扬了扬假眉毛,说:"猜猜我是谁!"

乔希瞪眼看着露丝,说:"多毛的公主?"

"不是。"

"格劳乔·马克斯[1]?"

她又摇了摇头。

"直接告诉我们吧,露丝。"丁丁说。

露丝做了个弹吉他的动作,大声说:"我是猫王埃尔维斯[2]!"

"我刚要猜他。"乔希说。

露丝看着他的那堆绿布条问:"你扮的是谁?"

乔希将绿布条缠到脸上,扮出个沼泽怪物的鬼脸。

"你猜。"他说。

露丝甜甜一笑:"你就是一块被撕成布条的绿床单。"

1.格劳乔·马克斯:美国喜剧演员、电影明星,主要作品有《疯狂的动物》等,有着浓密的眉毛和胡子。——译者

2.埃尔维斯:美国摇滚歌手,绰号"猫王"。——编者

门铃再次响起。

这一次，丁丁看见台阶上站着的是一个高个子男人。他穿着西装，打着领带，黑色鬈发，嘴唇上方蓄着小胡子，胡子两端向下垂着，下巴上有一道沟。

"嘿，你好。我是雷迪侦探，受雇于绿地储蓄银行，正在找人。你听说过那起抢劫案吗？"

乔希和露丝也来到丁丁身边。

丁丁点点头："我在电视上看到了新闻。"

"你是在找劫匪吗？"乔希问。

雷迪侦探摇摇头说："我在找见过他的人。当劫匪跑出银行时，他取下了面罩。当时有个孩子拿着录像机从旁边经过，将他拍了进去。银行雇我找到那个孩子，然后拿到录像带。"

"那个孩子长什么样？"露丝问。

雷迪侦探盯着她头上戴着的猫王式假发："银行里的人说他长着红头发，瘦高个。"

"听起来像你，乔希。"丁丁笑了起来，指着乔希的红头发说。

"不是我，我发誓！"乔希说，"我连录像机

都没有。"

"不是你，那个孩子比你大很多。"侦探说，"可能是个高中生。"他用手摸了摸自己的小胡子，"你们有谁认识那样的人吗？"

"不认识。"丁丁说，"但是我们很熟悉绿地镇，也许我们能帮您找到他。"

侦探看着三个孩子。

"我有个提议。"他开口道，"你们明天去高中查一查。如果你们找到那个拍摄到劫匪的男孩，拿到录像带，然后交给我，你们可以得到一笔相当丰厚的奖金。"

"多少钱？"乔希问。

"每人一百美元怎么样？"

"一百美元？"露丝激动得尖声叫了出来。

丁丁、乔希和雷迪侦探捂住了自己的耳朵。

"噢！"雷迪侦探说，"你的声音可真不小啊。"

"我们要是找到那个男孩，怎么联系您？"丁丁问。

侦探掏出便笺簿和铅笔，在一张纸上写了一行数字，然后将纸撕了下来。

光头劫匪

"这是我的电话号码,拿到录像带后就给我打电话。"

雷迪侦探走后,丁丁关上门。他笑得合不拢嘴,对乔希和露丝说:"每人一百美元!我们要发财了!"

第二章

"我有计划了。"丁丁说。

第二天下午三点左右,丁丁、乔希和露丝三人前往高中。绿地高中离绿地小学只有几个街区。

"乔希,你守在后门;露丝,你负责看着自行车停放架,但也要留心停车场。"

"我要怎么做到看着自行车停放架的同时,又留心停车场呢?"

"两只眼睛各看着一处。"乔希笑着说。

"你负责什么地方?"露丝问丁丁。

"我负责盯着前门。你们要是看到红头发的瘦男孩,拦住他,然后大叫。"

光头劫匪

露丝笑了起来:"拦住他,然后大叫?他会认为我们是疯子,然后逃走。"

"没错。"乔希说。

丁丁挠了挠他浓密的金发。"呃,好吧,别大叫,只需要问出他的姓名,告诉他,他有可能获得一笔钱。"

他们穿过高中旁边的公园。

"什么钱?"乔希问。

"如果我们找到录像带,雷迪会给我们每人一百美元,我觉得我们可以分一半给那个男孩,但他得向我们提供录像带才行。"

到了高中,他们分头行动。乔希绕到学校后门,露丝坐在自行车停放架旁边的草地上。

丁丁坐到了一条长椅上。这里视野很好,能清楚地看到前门。

突然,他听到一阵响亮的铃声。不一会儿,前门被猛地打开,一大群高中生推推搡搡挤过大门,争先恐后地跑下台阶。

丁丁站到长椅上,以免自己被人撞倒。他寻找着有红头发的男孩,但难度很大。有些学生戴

17

着帽子；有些学生穿着夹克或长袖运动衫，衣服帽子盖到了头上。丁丁有时甚至分辨不出他们是男孩还是女孩。

最后，他看见了一个高个子的红头发男孩。丁丁从长椅上跳了下来，向他追了过去。

"打扰一下。"丁丁喘着粗气说。

光头劫匪

"你是谁?"红头发男孩问。

"丁丁·邓肯。"丁丁努力回想自己计划好要说的话,"你或许可以获得一笔钱!"

红头发的男孩盯着丁丁,问:"钱?我?为什么?多少钱?"

"上周发生抢劫案时,你在银行附近吗?"他问。

男孩一直盯着丁丁,说:"抢劫案?什么抢劫案?"

"你没有听说吗?报纸和电视上都报道了。有人抢劫了绿地储蓄银行。"

"这和你有什么关系?"

"一个红头发男孩用录像机拍摄到了劫匪。"丁丁说,"我在帮人找他,找到他会有一笔奖金。"

"我倒是希望我拍到了劫匪,"红头发男孩摇着头说,"这样我就能得到奖金。但是上周我没去过银行附近。"他挥了挥手,往公园方向走去,"祝你好运!"

丁丁看向周围,寻找着别的红头发,但是人已经走光了。

他往自行车停放架走去。露丝正坐在草地上,无聊地将草叶子编成辫子。

"你看见有着红头发的人了吗?"丁丁问着,扑通一声,重重地坐到了露丝旁边。

"三个。"露丝说,"一个矮胖男孩,一个女孩,另一个是老师。"

乔希跑了过来。

"有什么发现吗?"他问。

"没有。"丁丁说,"你那边的情况呢?"

"我问了两个有着红头发的人。其中一个让我滚开;另一个是来自爱尔兰的交换生,他说他连银行在哪里都不知道。"

"很好。"丁丁说,"我们全都失败了。现在我们要怎么做?"

乔希朝着一棵树掷了一颗松果。"不知道。"

"我们应该把整个镇子都找一遍。"露丝说。

"怎么做?"丁丁问。

露丝站了起来,拍了拍自己短裤上的灰尘:"很容易,我们挨家挨户去问。"

"我们怎么做才能不让父母发现呢?"乔希问,

光头劫匪

"我父母肯定不会准许我被卷进银行抢劫案的。"

"我父母也不会准许。"丁丁说。

"那我们怎么解释自己在绿地镇挨家挨户敲人家的门呢?"乔希问。

"拜托,伙伴们,"露丝说,"想一想,今晚是什么?"

丁丁和乔希对视一眼。

"万圣夜!"

第三章

丁丁头发上涂着黑色鞋油，嘴里放着塑料尖牙，看起来像吸血鬼德古拉伯爵。

他妈妈用一件黑色的旧雨衣给他做了一件斗篷。他把斗篷系在脖子上时，门铃响了。

一个奇怪的东西站在门廊上。那东西裹着绿布，一簇簇红发从头顶的绿布中钻了出来，他的脚下是一双醒目的黑色大高帮鞋。

"我看起来怎么样？"那东西问。

丁丁取出嘴里的尖牙，露出一个大大的笑容："像怪异的蔬菜，有点像胡萝卜，也有点像芦笋。"

光头劫匪

乔希笨拙地走进屋里。

"你看起来不错,丁丁。我喜欢你嘴角那滴快要淌到下巴的血。"

门铃又响了。这次来的是迷你版的猫王。露丝身穿带有亮片的白色套装,背着一把小型吉他,她的猫王式假发让她看起来高了约两英寸[1]。

露丝弹了几下吉他,扭了扭屁股。

"非常感谢,女士们,先生们。"她说着,鞠了个躬。

"进来吧,猫王。"丁丁说,"在去索要糖果[2]前,我们必须先谈一谈我们的'红发行动'。"

他们在丁丁家厨房的餐桌边坐下,桌子上摆着一篮用来招待孩子们的糖果。

"以下是我的计划,"丁丁说,"我们挨家挨户地打听,看看他们是否认识一个有着红头发的瘦男孩。"

"这是我的计划!"露丝说。

---
1. 英寸:英美制长度单位。1 英寸 =2.54 厘米。——编者
2. 在万圣夜,孩子们会穿上各种奇异服装,挨家挨户地敲门向主人要糖果。——编者

丁丁笑了："哦，没错，我忘了。"

露丝的一条黑色眉毛歪了。"我们必须睁大眼睛，检查所有索要糖果的高个子孩子。"

"明白。"丁丁说。

"看见红头发的人，我们就问他是否拍摄到了银行劫匪。"露丝接着说。

"明白。"丁丁说，"还有别的吗？"

"有，我有个好主意。"乔希说，"我们回头再说，出发吧！"

丁丁的妈妈走进厨房。她捂住胸口惊叫起来。"噢,天哪!厨房里有怪物!"

露丝站了起来。"我不是怪物,邓肯太太,我是猫王!"

丁丁的妈妈帮露丝把左边的眉毛调正。"我知道,宝贝,你扮得真不错,但他们两个不行!"她身子一颤,做出个害怕的表情。

"我们现在就出发,妈妈。"丁丁将塑料尖牙套到牙齿上。他递给乔希一个纸袋,自己也拿了一个。

"两小时后一定要回来。"他妈妈说,"我和你爸爸会给你们准备好苹果汁和甜甜圈。"

三个孩子分别去了不同的街道,他们约定两个小时后回丁丁家集合。

丁丁沿着林荫街往前走。他注意着每一个穿着奇装异服的高个子孩子,查看他们是不是红头发,但大多数孩子都比他矮。他数了数,共发现十七个幽灵,二十个小女巫,八个垂着翅膀的天使,还有数不清的毛茸茸的小动物。

丁丁按响了戴维斯太太家的门铃。"不给糖就捣蛋!"

"哦,你好,丁丁!"戴维斯太太说着,往丁丁的纸袋里放了一小袋糖果。

"您今晚见过有着红头发的孩子吗?"丁丁问。

"红头发?"戴维斯太太摸了摸自己的头发,"除了你的好朋友乔希,我不认识有着红头发的孩子。"

丁丁向戴维斯太太道了谢,感谢她的糖果,然后来到隔壁的老克雷默先生家。

光头劫匪

克雷默先生的听力不太好。

"您认识有着红头发的瘦男孩吗?"丁丁大声问。

克雷默先生侧过脸,让自己的一只耳朵靠近丁丁。"你说什么?红色的小床?"

"红头发的男孩!"丁丁提高音量喊道。他真希望露丝也在这里,因为只有她的声音够大,大到能让克雷默先生听清。

克雷默先生往丁丁的袋子里放了一枚五分硬币,然后砰地关上了门。丁丁无奈地叹了口气。

丁丁跟着几个扮成幽灵的人来到林荫街的下一户人家。

丁丁按响门铃后,一只大猩猩打开了门。大猩猩有着毛茸茸的胸膛和满是黄色牙齿的大嘴。

"不给糖就捣蛋!"丁丁说。

大猩猩往丁丁的袋子里放了一根香蕉。

"你今天见过有着红头发的高个子青少年吗?"丁丁问。

大猩猩咕哝了一声,摇了摇头。

"还是谢谢你。"丁丁说。

两个小时后,丁丁、乔希、露丝将他们要到的糖果倒在了丁丁家的餐桌上。

丁丁取出他的尖牙。"有什么发现?"他问。

乔希将脸上的布条解开后说:"我看见了四个红头发的人:两个十来岁的女孩和两个成年人。所有我问过的人都说不认识读高中的有着红头发的瘦男孩。"

露丝取下假发,撕掉假眉毛,将它们扔进她的塑料南瓜灯里。

光头劫匪

"我这边的情况也一样。"露丝叹了口气,瘫坐到椅子上,"没人认识有着红头发的瘦男孩,我问了我见到的每一个人!"

乔希打开一小袋玛氏巧克力豆。

"虽然我真的很想要那一百美元,"他说,"但是也许我们该放弃了。"

"在努力了两天后放弃?不可能,伙伴们!"丁丁爬上桌子,用斗篷包着脸,只露出一双眼睛。

他尽力模仿着吸血鬼德古拉伯爵的声音说:"我们永不放弃!"

第四章

第二天早上,丁丁的头发因涂抹过黑色鞋油而变得根根僵直。他洗澡时用洗发水洗了三遍。

他想照一下镜子,但浴室的镜子起了雾。他擦了一下镜子,看到镜子中的自己时,惊得倒吸了一口凉气。

他的头发不是平常的金色,也不是吸血鬼的黑色,而是泥浆般的棕色,与他自行车上的铁锈颜色一样。

"妈妈!帮帮我!"

他妈妈向浴室里看了一眼:"怎么……噢,我明白了。"她咯咯地笑了起来。

光头劫匪

"妈妈,这一点都不好笑。这样我怎么出门?我的头发看起来像生了锈。"

"宝贝,今天一定有很多孩子的脸上都留有化妆品的痕迹,或者头发上残留着其他颜色,因为昨晚是万圣夜。"

丁丁使劲用毛巾擦着头发。他照了照镜子,发现头发变成了铁锈色的鬈发。

"幸好今天是周六。"他妈妈笑着说,"至少你今天不用去上学。"

吃完早餐,丁丁把棒球帽往头发上一扣,朝乔希家走去。

丁丁到那儿时,乔希正在谷仓前练习投篮。他对着丁丁咧嘴笑了。

"你的头发怎么了?"他问。

丁丁扯下帽子说:"你看,这鞋油怎么都洗不掉。我只能扮吸血鬼了,对吧?扮不了牛仔或宇航员。"

乔希运球投篮,但球没进。

"关于寻找那个拿着录像带的男孩,你想出什么新计划了吗?"乔希问。

"没有。"丁丁说着,又把帽子扣回头上。

"那么,我们现在该怎么做?"乔希问,"继续挨家挨户地问吗?"

"我也不知道。"丁丁说,"万圣夜已经过去了,继续那么做的话,我们看上去会相当可疑。另外,绿地镇有上百栋住宅,我们走完要一个月的时间。"

乔希再次投篮,球顺利进了。"两分!"

"我们应该用脑想,而不是用脚走。"丁丁说着,在乔希投篮得分后接住了球。

他们身后的一扇门砰地打开了。

"哎呀。"乔希咕哝了一声。

"乔希,我们该走了。"乔希的妈妈喊道,"进来刷牙吧。"

"我约了去看牙医。"乔希说,"晚些时候给我打电话,好吗?"

"好的。"丁丁将乔希的篮球扔进谷仓,抬脚准备离开。

"喂!"乔希在他身后喊道,"我觉得你头发的新颜色看起来很可爱!"

光头劫匪

"很可笑。"丁丁嘀咕着,用力把帽子往下拉了拉。

"也许,我应该把头发剪了,"他想,"周一顶着个光头去上学。"

突然,他停下了脚步。

想到剪头发,他突然有了主意。

他朝着主街跑去。到了霍华德理发店,他透过玻璃窗仔细向店内看去。霍华德正在看电视,小型电视机屏幕上正在重播《我爱露西》。

丁丁走了进去,门口的雪橇铃响了起来。每次他来这里理发,都会想起圣诞节。

"今天想要什么样的发型,丁丁?"霍华德问,"想理平头吗?莫霍克发型怎么样?中间留有一道头发的那种?"

"我不想理发,"丁丁说,"我来找您问点事。"

霍华德眯起他的一只蓝色眼睛,拿下丁丁的棒球帽,问:"你的头发怎么了?"

丁丁脸红了:"我昨晚扮成了吸血鬼,在头发上抹了黑色的鞋油,后来怎么洗也洗不干净。我试了各种方法。"

33

　　霍华德笑着说:"坐到椅子上去,孩子。我给你用一下我的特制洗发水。有什么事你可以在我表演'魔术'的过程中再问。"

　　丁丁把帽子挂在挂钩上,爬上了理发椅。霍华德从柜子里拿出一只瓶子和几条毛巾。

　　"我想问您是否认识有着红头发的孩子,"丁

丁说,"乔希除外。"

　　霍华德将一条毛巾披在丁丁的肩膀上,用别针在后面别住,然后拿起装着水的喷壶将丁丁的头发打湿。

　　"可能认识。"他回答,"你是想让我把你的头发染红吗?"

丁丁笑了起来："不是，我正在找一个有着红头发的孩子。我想他是个十几岁的青少年。"

"我认识一个曾经有着红头发的青少年。"霍华德一边说，一边将绿色的洗发水倒到丁丁的头发上，"但他的红头发在上周被我剃掉了。他激动地跑到这里，气喘吁吁地对我说：'剃掉我的头发！'于是我照做了。"

洗发水的气味熏得丁丁直流眼泪。他觉得自己的心跳在加快。

"他当时拿着录像机吗？"丁丁问。

霍华德将洗发水揉进丁丁的头发里。

"你为什么对这个有着红头发的男孩这么感兴趣？"他问。

丁丁思考了片刻，决定和盘托出。他对霍华德说了银行抢劫案的事，包括银行劫匪、拿着录像机的孩子和侦探承诺的三百美元。

霍华德轻声笑了："哦，现在我终于知道，那个男孩为什么跑到这里大声叫着要我剃掉他的头发了。他不想让那个劫匪认出他来。如果我告诉你那个男孩的姓名，你要去说服他把录像带交给你吗?"

"是的,要是有机会的话。"丁丁说。

"那钱呢?"霍华德问。

丁丁看向镜子中的霍华德:"钱怎么啦?"

"你打算与那个有着红头发的男孩分享那笔奖金吗?"

丁丁笑着说:"当然,侦探给我们的奖金可以分他一半。"

"听起来不错。"霍华德用力揉搓着丁丁的头发。丁丁通过镜子看着,发现自己的头发变成了一团黏糊糊的、绿色的东西。

"这东西真的能把鞋油弄掉吗?"他问。

"能,我自己研制的,"霍华德说,"是我的秘方。我曾用它将我孙女头发上的泡泡糖洗掉了,还用它去掉了我家狗身上的沥青。"

霍华德将理发椅转过来,放下椅背,把丁丁的头放到水槽上方。

"闭上眼睛,孩子。我们来把这黏糊糊的东西洗掉,看看效果如何。"

丁丁喜欢温水冲洗的感觉,喜欢霍华德用手

指揉搓他的头发，将头发漂洗干净。几分钟后，霍华德将椅背立起来，然后抛了条干净的毛巾到丁丁头上。

"擦干。我想你的头发颜色恢复了。"

丁丁用毛巾擦干头发，然后看向镜子。他哈哈大笑起来："确实有效！"

霍华德微笑着看向镜子里的丁丁："我应该把这东西拿出去卖，挣个上百万美元。"

"我该付多少钱？"丁丁问。

"这次算我请客，小伙子。那个红头发的男孩就是奥利里家的幸运儿。他和母亲、弟弟妹妹们住在知更鸟路。他一共有六个弟弟妹妹！孩子们都不错，每个都有着红头发。"

霍华德将座椅调低，笑着说："除了那个突然决定要剃光头的幸运儿。"

第五章

"他成了光头?"乔希一边问,一边走上露丝家门前的台阶。

丁丁从理发店直接跑回家,给乔希打了电话。现在他们要找露丝,然后一起去知更鸟路。

"霍华德是这么说的。"丁丁对乔希说。丁丁按响了门铃。

"怪不得我们在高中没有找到他!"乔希说。

"请进!"露丝在屋里高声喊道。

露丝正坐在地上与她四岁的弟弟纳特一起看录像。

"快点,露丝。我们找到那个有着红头发的

男孩了！"丁丁说，"我们要去他家。"

露丝跳了起来，大声喊道："我要和朋友们出去，妈妈！您看好纳特！"

丁丁和乔希捂住耳朵。

露丝对纳特说："你乖乖待着，等妈妈来，好不好？"

纳特点点头，眼睛没有从电视机屏幕上移开。

"我们走！"露丝带头向门外走去，跳下了门前的台阶。

"你们是怎么找到那个男孩的？"她问。

丁丁把自己无法洗掉头发上的鞋油的事说了一遍。

"那让我想要把头发剪掉，于是我想起了理发店。谁会认识镇里所有有着红头发的人呢？"

"理发师霍华德！"露丝尖声叫道。

两个男孩再次捂住了他们的耳朵。

"我以后一定会和老克雷默先生一样，需要佩戴助听器。"乔希嘀咕道。

丁丁在电话号码簿上查到了奥利里家在知更鸟路的住址。他们来到33号住宅前。这是一栋

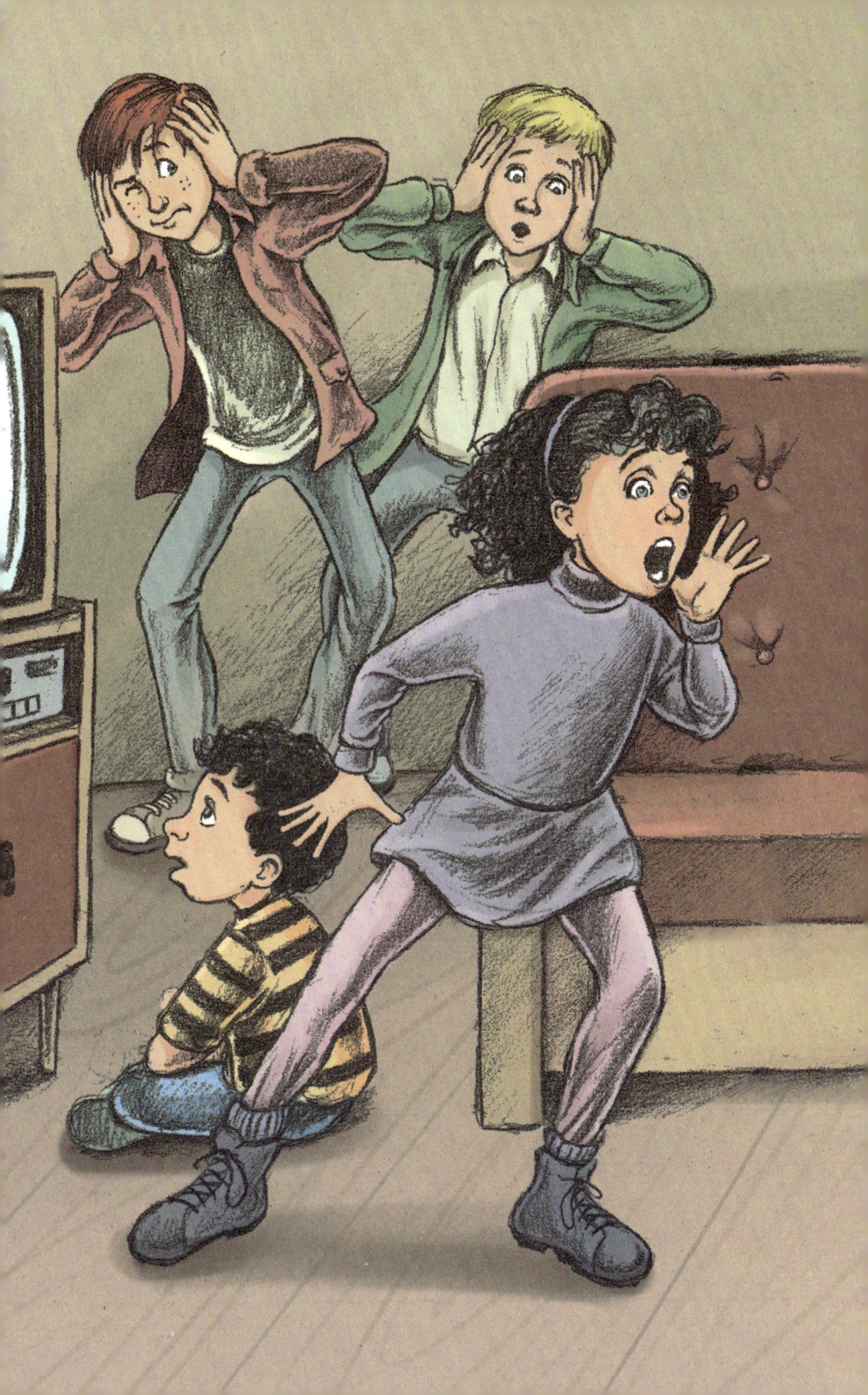

蓝色的大房子，玩具、自行车、运动鞋和篮球杂乱地扔在草坪上。嘈杂的音乐声从前门传了出来。

他们走上门廊，跨过了一根棒球棍。四个南瓜灯排成一排，上面都雕刻着吓人的面孔。

丁丁按响门铃。"祈求好运吧。"他说。

开门的是一个小女孩。她一头红头发，脸上满是雀斑。

"嘿！我是约瑟芬，我五岁半了！"她伸出了十根手指。

"你哥哥在家吗？"丁丁问。

"哪一个？我有这么多哥哥！"约瑟芬再次伸出十根手指。

丁丁笑了起来："你是不是有个叫幸运儿的哥哥？"

音乐声停了。

"是谁在外面，小芬？"一个身穿破牛仔裤和T恤衫的瘦高个青少年走过来问道。丁丁注意到他头顶有一层红色的茸毛，就像是新长出来的红色草坪。

"你是幸运儿奥利里吗？"丁丁问。

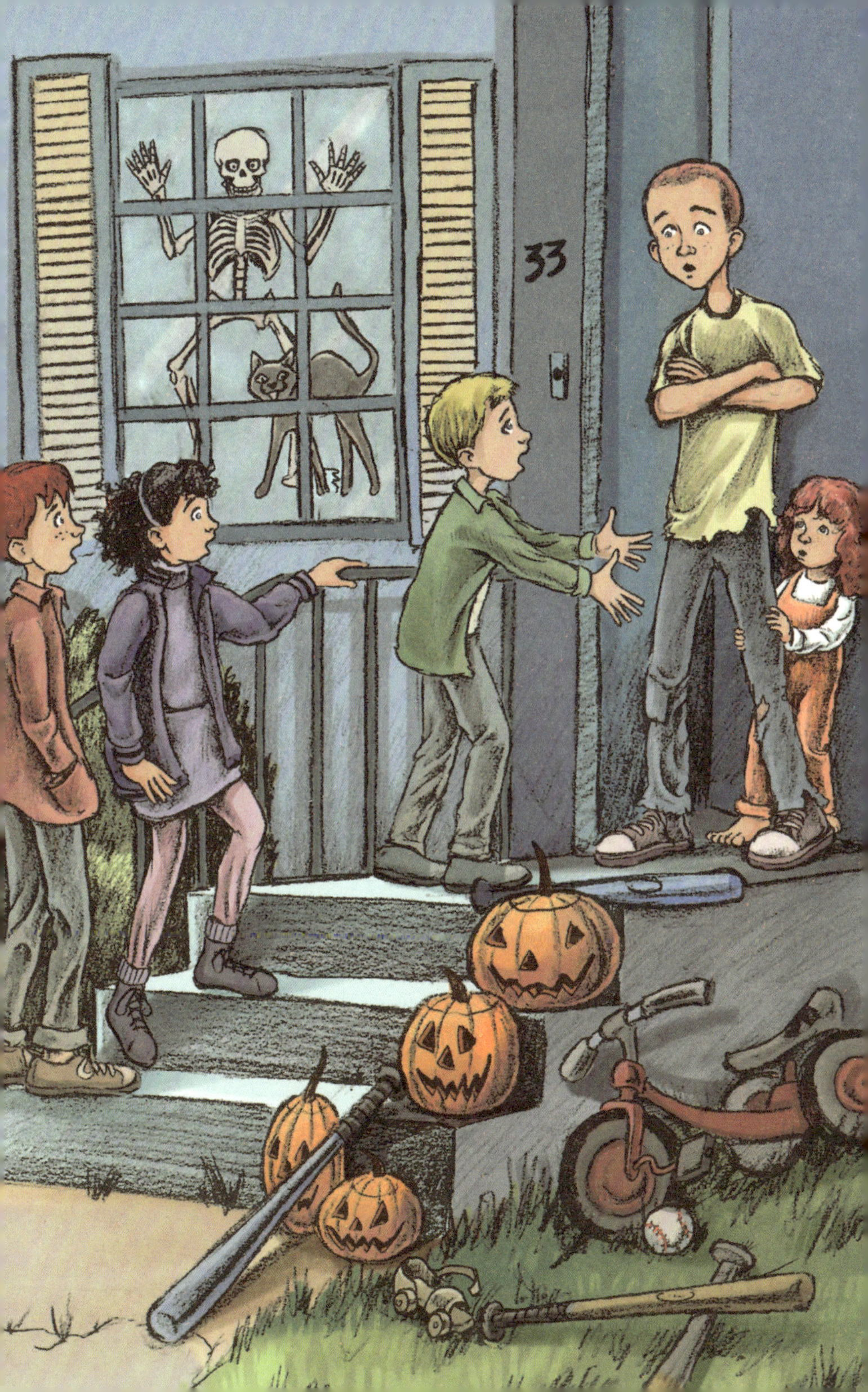
33

那个男孩低头看向丁丁、乔希和露丝:"是谁要找他?"

"我们。"露丝回答,"你想挣一笔钱吗?"

"也许。"他说。

"我们正在找一个男孩,他上周拍摄到了抢劫绿地储蓄银行的劫匪。"丁丁说,"银行请了一个侦探寻找录像带,而我们在帮侦探寻找。如果我们找到录像带,他会付钱给我们,到时我们可以将钱分给你一半——如果你就是那个男孩。"

"你是吗?"露丝问。

那个男孩摸了摸头上的红色茸毛。"是的,"他咕哝道,"我就是。"

然后,他交叉着抱起双臂,说:"但是,我是不会把录像带交给侦探的。"

第六章

孩子们睁大眼睛看着幸运儿。

"为什么不呢?"露丝问,"那个侦探在帮银行抓捕劫匪。你可以成为英雄!"

"嘘!"幸运儿紧张地四下看了看,然后示意丁丁、乔希和露丝进屋。

"快进来。"

走进屋里,孩子们跟着幸运儿沿着走廊进入他的卧室。丁丁注意到他走路有点一瘸一拐的。他卧室的墙上贴满了篮球明星的海报,地上到处扔着衣服。

幸运儿一屁股坐到床上。

"听着,"他说,"我不敢将录像带交给侦探。如果那个劫匪发现是我交出去的,会怎么样?以我这倒霉运气,他一定会来找我的。"

"劫匪怎么会知道是你录的像?"丁丁问。

幸运儿坐了起来。"因为他跑出银行时正好看到了我。那个家伙看见我正在拍他!这也是我跑到霍华德理发店将头发剃光的原因。"幸运儿在他毛茸茸的头上挠了挠。

"如果你把录像带交出来,那个劫匪就会被抓,你根本不用担心。"乔希说。

"此外,我们会分给你一半的奖金。"露丝说,"对吧,伙伴们?"

"对。"丁丁说,"幸运儿是你的真名吗?"

那个男孩摇摇头说:"我的真名叫保罗,幸运儿是我的绰号。别人这么叫我是因为我运气奇差。自从开学以后,我的狗死了,我的自行车被偷了,我的脚趾断了,我几乎无法步行去学校。"

"你可以用这笔奖金买一辆新的自行车。"露丝说,"这样你就不用走路了。"

幸运儿看着露丝笑了笑。"我正在为上大学

攒钱。"他说着,叹了一口气,"我好像总是很缺钱。"

幸运儿考虑了片刻。

"听着,那笔奖金对我真的有用。"他说,"但是,你们几个必须承诺,不说出是谁提供的录像带。"

孩子们点头同意。

"那好。"幸运儿说。他下了床,一瘸一拐地走到衣橱前,从最上面的一层取下一只盒子,盒子里装着一些录像带。他将其中的一盘递给丁丁。

幸运儿看起来有点尴尬。"呃……我什么时候能拿到钱?"他问。

"也许明天。"丁丁说,"我们会及时联系你的,好吗?"

"好的,没问题。"幸运儿说,他做了个封口的动作,"记住,你们已经答应了我,不告诉任何人你们是从哪里拿到录像带的,连那个侦探也不能告诉。"

孩子们再次点点头。

幸运儿送他们到门口，绕过了一群在客厅地板上扭打的孩子。丁丁注意到他们都长着红头发和雀斑。

约瑟芬从人堆中探出头来。

"再见!"她笑着向丁丁道别。

丁丁、乔希和露丝三人走到人行道上,互相击掌庆贺。

"我们终于拿到了!"乔希大声叫道。

丁丁将录像带塞进口袋:"我们现在只要给雷迪侦探打个电话,就能拿到奖金了!"

第七章

孩子们急忙赶回丁丁家。家里没人，丁丁用钥匙打开了前门。

他看见厨房餐桌上有一张便条，上面写着：

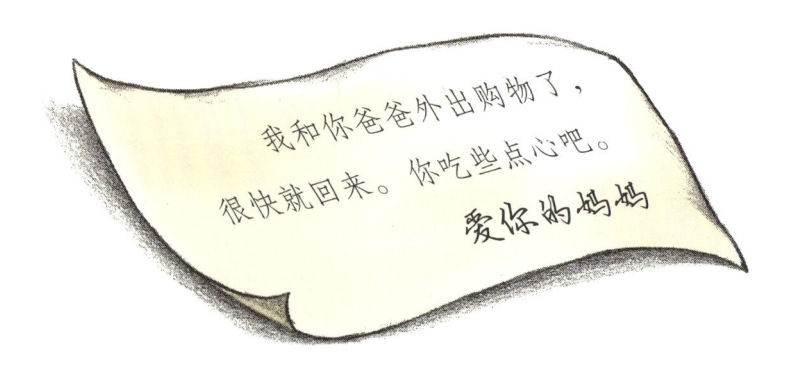

> 我和你爸爸外出购物了，很快就回来。你吃些点心吧。
>
> 爱你的妈妈

光头劫匪

丁丁很高兴爸爸妈妈都不在家,因为他知道,他们不会喜欢他玩侦探游戏。等事情结束后,他再告诉他们,他是如何挣到一百美元的。

乔希打开冰箱。"你家有什么吃的?"他问。

丁丁将录像带放在柜台上。"柜台上应该有甜甜圈。"

他从口袋里掏出那张写有侦探电话号码的字条,然后拨了号码。

"喂,是雷迪侦探吗?我是丁丁·邓肯。我和我的朋友们帮您找到了录像带。什么?没有,我们没有看录像带里的内容。好的,再见。"

丁丁挂上电话,笑着说:"他马上过来。他说我们是了不起的侦探,并且让我们不要看录像带里的内容。"

乔希正吃着甜甜圈。"为什么不让看?"他问道,嘴里塞满了食物。

"他说这是最高机密。"

他们你看看我,我看看你。

"快来!"丁丁说着,一把抓起录像带。

他们跑进客厅。丁丁将电视机打开,将录像

51

带插入录像机。

录像的开始部分是一只大狗咬着一根橡胶骨头。然后,他们看见一个穿着泳衣的女孩笑着躲避镜头。接下来是在一个生日聚会上,里面多数人长得和幸运儿奥利里很像。丁丁认出了小约瑟芬。

最后,他们看见了绿地储蓄银行的前门。门开了,一个男人跑出来,将脸上的滑雪面罩摘了

下来。

"这一定就是那个劫匪!"丁丁说着,按了暂停键。

录像带上的男人是个光头,他的光头在太阳下闪闪发亮。他穿着运动裤和运动衫,背着一个健身包,脸上一副震惊的表情。

"他一定是在这时注意到幸运儿在拍他的。"乔希说。

露丝走近电视机。"看，他下巴上有一道沟。"

突然，露丝惊得倒吸了一口气。她跑出客厅，跑到屋外，房门在她身后砰地关上了。

丁丁看向乔希："出了什么事？"

乔希耸耸肩说："也许她不喜欢下巴上有沟的人。"

过了一会儿，房门猛地打开了，露丝又跑了回来。她手里拿着她那猫王式的假发和假眉毛。

露丝将一条假眉毛粘在电视屏幕上劫匪的鼻子下方，就像是一撇小胡子。然后，她又把假发放在劫匪的光头上。

"看起来像谁？"她问。

乔希跳了起来，惊呼："噢，天哪！这个劫匪长得和雷迪侦探一模一样！"

正在这时，门铃响了！丁丁从前窗往外看去。

"是谁？"乔希问。

丁丁转过身来，双眼圆睁："是雷迪侦探！"

第八章

露丝一把将假发和假眉毛从电视机上扯下来，藏在背后。

乔希按下"弹出"按钮，将录像带退了出来，塞进自己的衬衫。

丁丁盯着大门，觉得自己都不会走路了。

门铃再次响起。

丁丁看向他的两个朋友，然后深吸一口气，打开了门。

露丝在雷迪侦探进来时，偷偷溜了出去。

"嘿，你们好。"雷迪侦探笑容满面地与丁丁和乔希打招呼，"哇，你们几个真聪明。你们是怎么找到那个录像的红头发孩子的？"

丁丁瞪着面前的男人，几乎不敢相信，雷迪侦探根本就不是一个侦探，而是一个银行劫匪！而且他现在正站在丁丁家的客厅里！

"我猜，我们只是运气好点。"丁丁嘟囔道。

男人摸了摸自己的小胡子。"东西在哪里？"

丁丁不想让他看到乔希衬衫里隆起的东西："什么东西在哪里？"

"录像带，你在电话中说拿到了录像带。现在录像带在哪里？"

丁丁的脑子一片空白，他不知道该怎么回答。

"想一想，丁丁！"他命令自己。

乔希急忙救场："我们把录像带藏到了楼上，记得吗，丁丁？"

丁丁看向乔希："嗯？哦，没错，我想起来了。"他笑着对男人说："我们想确保将它交给您之前，没人看见它。"

"快点，丁丁。"乔希朝着楼梯走去。

"拿一盘录像带需要你们两个人一起去吗？"男人问。

"呃……放在我妈妈的房间里了。"丁丁举起他家前门的钥匙,"只有我才能打开房间。"

丁丁急急忙忙跟在乔希后面上了楼。他们跑进丁丁的卧室,关上了房门。

丁丁的豚鼠洛蕾塔吱吱地叫了起来,在笼子里跑来跑去。

"现在不是玩的时候,洛蕾塔。"丁丁说。

"露丝去哪里了?"乔希问,"我不敢相信她竟然抛弃了我们!"

丁丁没有回答。他在床前走来走去,拽着自己的头发,紧张地打着响指。

"丁丁,别走了,你走得我有点头晕。"乔希说,"我们要怎么做?"

丁丁停下脚步。"我也不知道!我们不能把录像带交给他,因为他会毁了它,那样的话,证据就没有了!他会逍遥法外的。他甚至会去找幸运儿的麻烦!"

"我们必须抓住他,把他交给警察。"乔希说,"你有绳子吗?我们扑上去,把他捆起来!"

"我房间里没有绳子,乔希。"丁丁说,"另外,

他比我们高大,力气也更大,他可能还有枪!"

"你们需要我帮忙吗?"那个男人高声喊道。

丁丁将门开了一条缝。"不用,我们马上下来。"

丁丁从他的书架上拿起一盘足球赛录像带,递给乔希:"我们把这个给他。"

"但是,当他发现这不是那盘录像带,会怎

么样?"乔希问。

"不知道,但我们没有其他选择。"

乔希将幸运儿的那盘录像带拿出来,放到洛蕾塔的笼子里,用刨花将它盖好。

"守好它,洛蕾塔。"他说。

他们下了楼。丁丁努力扯出一个微笑。

"我们找到了！"他说。

乔希将足球赛录像带递给了他。

正在此时，前门突然开了，露丝出现了，身旁是绿地警察局的法伦警官和基恩警官。

丁丁见到他们，惊喜万分。

"就是他！"露丝说着，指向拿着录像带的男人，"他抢了绿地储蓄银行！"

两位警官走进客厅。

那个男人笑着说："我是私家侦探，警官。"

"能否出示一下您的证件，先生？"法伦警官说。

那个男人摸了摸他的小胡子，"我没带钱包。"

"是吗？"基恩警官说，"侦探需要随身携带证件。"

"是的，我一般都带着，今天我把钱包忘在车里了。我去取，马上回来。"

"他的胡子是假的！"露丝走到警官跟前说，"头发也是假的！"

每个人都看着那个男人。

突然,那个男人一把抓起露丝,把她挡在身前。

"让开!"他大声叫道,"我要离开,带着这个女孩一起离开!"

露丝深吸了一口气。

然后,她以前所未有的洪亮的声音尖叫起来。

"啊——"

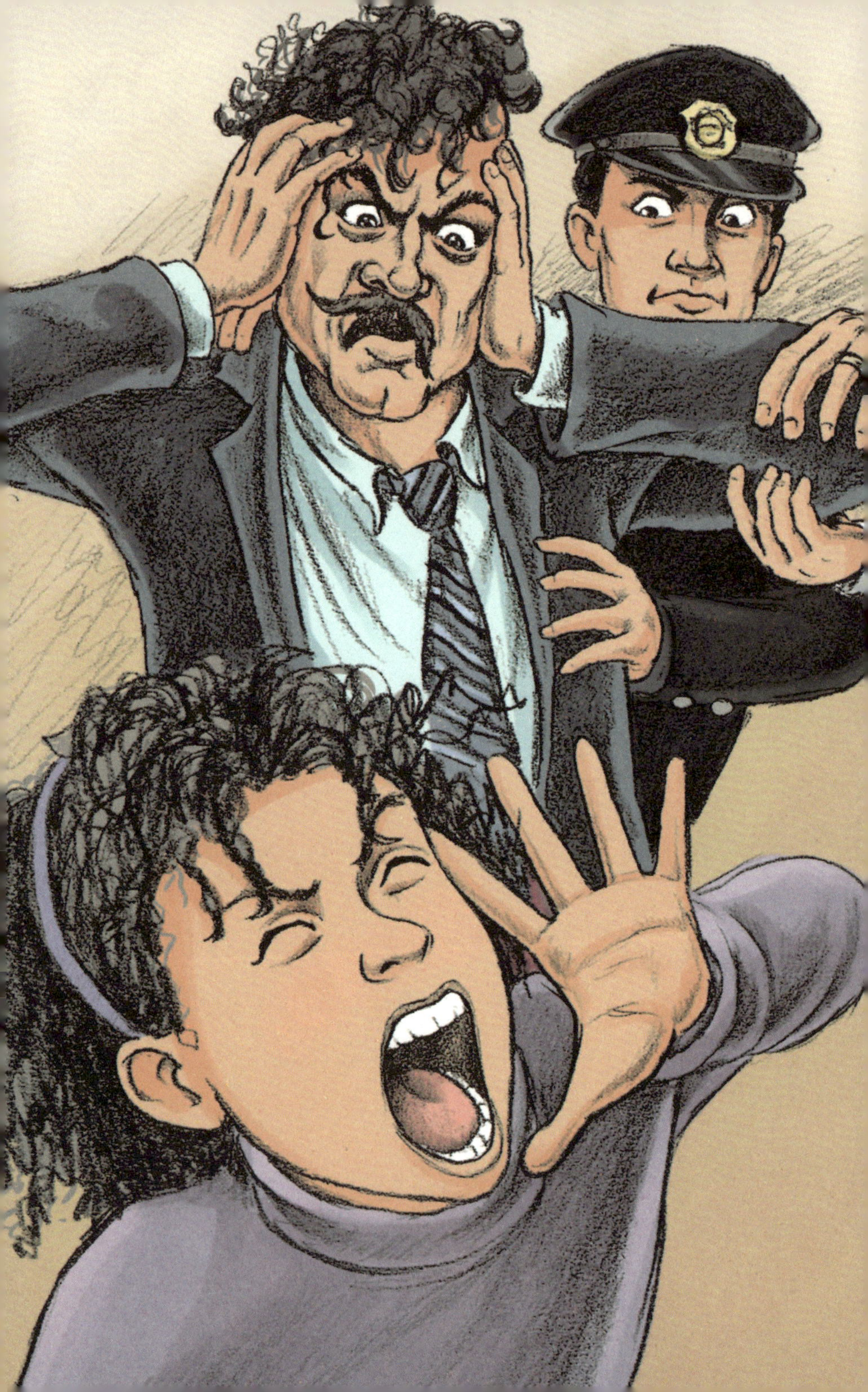

第九章

乔希、丁丁和警官们都捂住了自己的耳朵。

"哎哟!"银行劫匪叫了一声。

他向后踉跄几步,也用双手捂住了自己的耳朵。

他一放开露丝,法伦警官就抓住了他。

"一切都结束了,伙计。"法伦警官说着,把手铐铐在了那个男人的手腕上。

基恩警官撕下劫匪的假胡子和假发。那个男

人现在看上去和他在录像带里的样子完全一样：光头闪闪发亮，脸上一副震惊的表情。

基恩警官把他带了出去。

法伦警官将手放到露丝的肩膀上。"露丝，你没事吧？"

露丝点点头："我没事，法伦警官。"

"那你和我说的录像带在哪里？"

乔希跑上楼，取出幸运儿的录像带。他回到客厅，将录像带插入录像机。他们看录像时，丁丁告诉了法伦警官事情的经过。

法伦警官笑着说："我们的劫匪相当狡猾。他雇你们去寻找拍到他的样貌的录像带。如果让他毁掉了录像带，就没人能证明他曾去过那家银行了。"

"他无法自己去寻找录像带，"露丝解释道，"因为那个男孩可能会认出他，就像我认出他一样。"

"你们是怎么拿到这盘录像带的？"法伦警官问。

丁丁没有忘记他们对幸运儿的承诺："我们不能说出我们是从哪里得到的，我们答应过别人。"

法伦警官笑着说:"好吧,抓到录像带上的人应该得到奖赏。说起这个,我想你们几个会得到银行给予的一笔五千美元的奖金。"

"五千美元!"乔希从座位上跳了起来。他和丁丁高兴得在客厅跳起舞来。

法伦警官大笑着说:"露丝是个勇敢的孩子,她偷偷溜回家打电话,报了警。"

露丝的脸变成了她最喜欢的粉红色。

法伦警官离开后,露丝用丁丁的计算器算了一下。"我们分给幸运儿一半后,每个人能分得八百三十三点三三美元,之后还余一美分。"她说。

"我们发财了!"乔希说,"我们使劲花吧!"

丁丁笑着说:"我的钱要存入我的储蓄账户。"

"我的也是。"露丝说,"我要存钱买电脑。"

乔希瘫倒在椅子上,说:"好吧,你们是对的,如果我在比萨和冰激凌上挥霍掉八百美元,我家人一定不会饶过我。"

周一,绿地小学一放学,丁丁、乔希和露丝就跑去了高中。他们气喘吁吁地坐在高中前面的一张长椅上。

"你告诉幸运儿他能得到五千美元的一半时,他说了什么?"乔希问。

"什么也没说,"丁丁笑着说,"因为我还没告诉他。"

这时,铃声响了。片刻之后,孩子们如潮水般从学校涌出。

"他在那里!"露丝朝幸运儿跑过去,领着他来到长椅边。幸运儿的脸上满是笑容。

"露丝说你们拿到奖金了。你们把我的一百五十美元带来了吗?"他问。

丁丁愁眉苦脸地摇摇头,说:"并没有。"

"'并没有'是什么意思?"

三个好朋友哈哈大笑起来。

"我们没有带来一百五十美元,但我们带来了这个。"丁丁说。

他递给幸运儿一张两千五百美元的支票。

幸运儿瞠目结舌,嘴巴都合不上了。"两千五百美元!"他大声叫道,"这是哪儿来的?"

"这是你的那一半奖金,银行发的。"丁丁说,"我们回家后看了你的那盘录像带。露丝认出了那个劫匪。原来他就是那个侦探,但他并不是真正的侦探,只是扮作侦探,这样他就能够找到你,并拿走录像带。"

幸运儿眨了眨眼:"所以你们抓住了他?"

"没错,就在丁丁家里抓住了他!"乔希说,"露丝偷偷溜了出去,打电话报了警。"

"真是惊险!"露丝说。

幸运儿再次看向他的那张支票,摇着头,笑得合不拢嘴:"今天是我的幸运日。现在我妈妈有钱给所有的孩子买学习用品了,也可以把车修好了。"

"上大学呢?"丁丁问,"我还以为那是这笔钱的用处。"

幸运儿摇了摇头。"现在还不是上大学的时候。我必须先工作一段时间,等我和妈妈挣到更多的钱再说。"幸运儿看着支票说,"也许是明年。"

他与三个孩子握手道别:"无论如何,感谢你们给我这张支票,我等不及要看看我妈妈见到这张支票后的高兴模样了。"

A to Z 神秘案件

丁丁看着幸运儿走远,今天他好像瘸得没有那么厉害了。

"我很好奇,用我的八百三十三点三三美元,幸运儿能买几门课程。"丁丁说。

露丝微笑着看向丁丁:"我很好奇,他用我的那一笔钱可以买多少本书。"

乔希睁大了眼睛,惊讶地说:"什么?你们要把自己的钱给幸运儿?那是你们挣的!"

丁丁摇了摇头,说:"不,不是我们挣的。我们只是跑去向人打听消息,幸运儿才是应该挣到这笔奖金的人。"

"没错,"露丝也说,"他才是拍摄到劫匪的人。"

丁丁和露丝向主街走去。

"喂,你们去哪儿?"乔希大声问。

"去银行。"丁丁回头说,"然后去幸运儿家。"

露丝转身看向乔希:"你和我们一起去吗?"

乔希咧嘴笑了,追上丁丁和露丝。"我很好奇,用我的八百三十三点三三美元,幸运儿能在大学食堂买多少顿饭。"他说。

光头劫匪

"我们比赛,看谁先跑到银行吧!"露丝提议。三个好朋友快跑起来。

A to Z Mysteries®

The Bald Bandit

by **Ron Roy**

illustrated by
John Steven Gurney

INDIAN RIVER
LAWRENCE TAXI
RIVER ROAD
HORSE TRAILS
HORSES FOR RENT
BIKE PATH
WOODS
INDIAN WAY ROAD
WOODVIEW ROAD
FIRE STATION
BILL'S BIKES
SUPER MARKET
BIKE PATH
BRIDGE LANE
ROBIN ROAD
CROW ST
FINCH LA
THRUSH CT
OWL RD
PHEASANT LA
BLUE JAY WAY
WREN DR
FITNESS CENTER
WOODS
BIKE PATH
BLUE BIRD WAY
HUMMINGBIRD LA
WOODCOCK CROSS
ELLIE'S DINER
ACORN APTS
FURRY FEET PET SHOP
OAK STREET
CENTER CHURCH
BIKE PATH
PEOPLE'S POND
POST OFFICE
COMMUNITY GARDEN AND FISH POND
GREEN LAWN $ SAVINGS BANK $
ELDERLY HOUSING
POLICE STATION
WEST GREEN ST
GOOSE ISLAND
RIVER ROAD
MAIN STREET
SENIOR COMMUNITY CENTER
GREEN LAWN LIBRARY
TOWN HALL
BIKE PATH
CHILDREN'S PETTING ZOO AND AQUARIUM
SHANGRI-LA HOTEL

WELCOME TO
GREEN LAWN
HOME OF THE
A to Z Mysteries
N
W
E
S
RIVER ROAD
BOAT LAUNCH
BOAT RENTAL
RON'S BAIT
DUCK WALK WAY
GREEN LAWN MIDDLE SCHOOL
EAGLE LANE
FARM LANE
JOSH
SQUAW ISLAND
GREEN LAWN ELEMENTARY SCHOOL
DINK
RUTH ROSE
TREE TOP CIRCLE
MEADOW ROAD
FOX LANE
QUAIL RUN ROAD
SILVER CIRCLE
WOODY STREET
PLEASANT STREET
BAND SHELL
ROSE GARDEN
THISTLE COURT
WILDFLOWER WAY
ROSE STREET
CENTER PARK
SWAN POND
GREEN LAWN HIGH SCHOOL
PLAYING FIELDS
GYM + POOL
BOXWOOD LANE
HOWARD'S BARBER-SHOP
BOOK NOOK
GAS STATION
CRYSTAL POND
MYSTIC GREENHOUSE
DOG KENNEL + VETERINARIAN
RIVER ROAD
EAST GREEN STREET
TOWN TENNIS COURTS
TOWN SWIMMING POOL
KIDDIE POOL
TOWN BASEBALL FIELD
TO THE BLUE HILLS

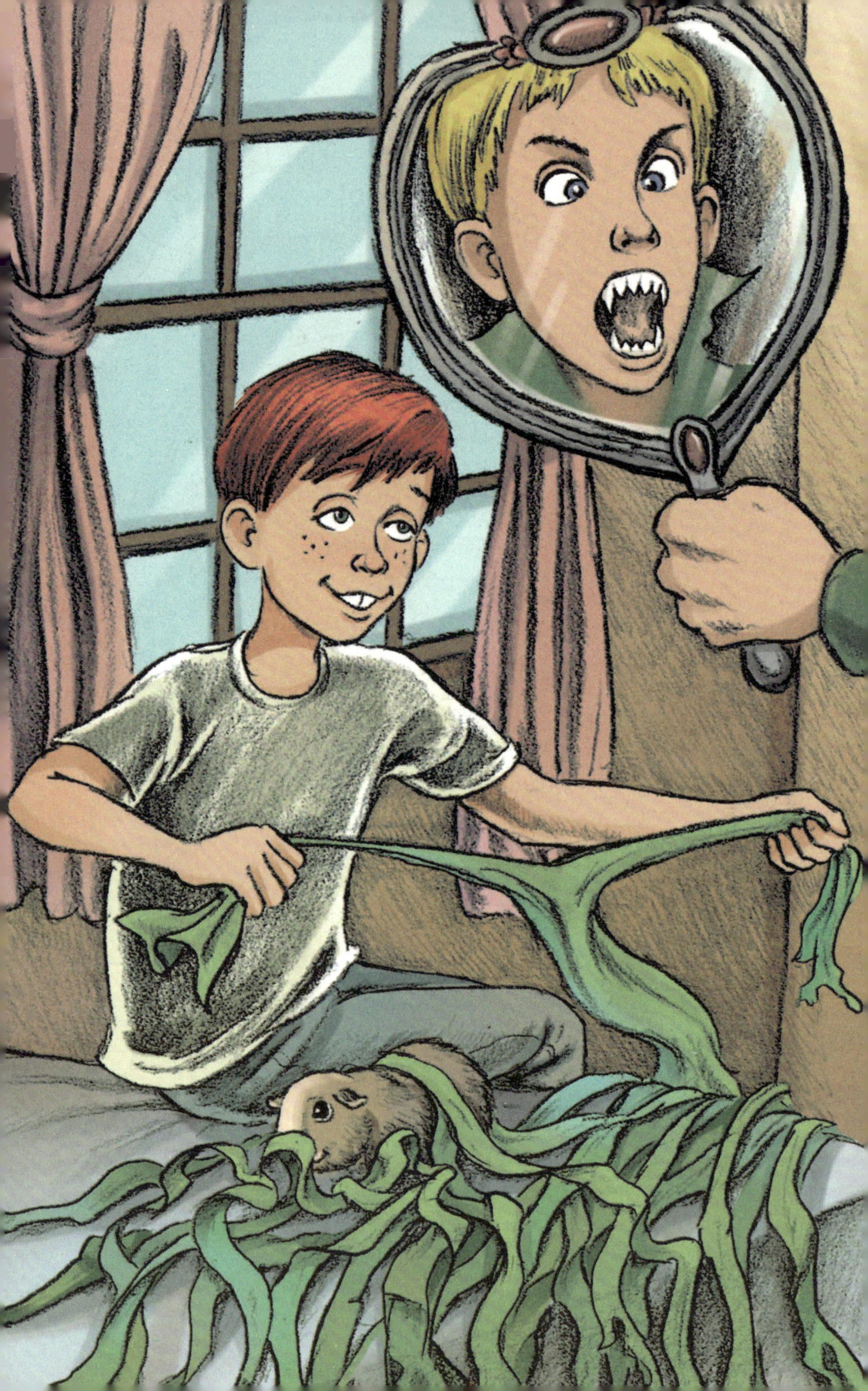

Chapter 1

Dink slipped the plastic fangs into his mouth. He made a scary face at his best friend, Josh Pinto.

"Do I look like a vampire?" It was hard to talk without spitting, so Dink took the fangs out again.

Dink's full name was Donald David Duncan, but nobody called him Donald. Except his mom, when she was upset. Then she called him by all three names.

Josh grinned. "No. You look like a skinny third-grader wearing false teeth."

"Wait till I put on the rest of my costume," Dink said. "Then I'll look like a vampire."

"Maybe you will." Josh was tearing a green bedsheet into long strips. "And maybe you won't."

Dink's guinea pig, Loretta, crawled among the green strips. Every now and then she let out a curious squeak.

"How will you be able to walk if you're wrapped up in all those strips?" Dink asked Josh.

Josh kept tearing. "Swamp monsters don't walk," he said in a slithery voice. "They gliiiide."

"Okay, so how will you be able to gliiiide wrapped up in all those strips?"

The doorbell rang. When Dink opened the door, his next-door neighbor, Ruth Rose, was standing on the steps.

"Hi, Ruth Rose. Why are you wearing a wig? Halloween isn't until tomorrow."

Ruth Rose was dressed in her usual bright

clothes—a pink shirt, pink pants, and pink sneakers. But on her head she wore a shiny black wig. She also had on thick fake eyebrows.

Ruth Rose wiggled the fake eyebrows up and down. "Guess who I am!"

Josh stared at Ruth Rose. "A hairy princess?"

"No."

"Groucho Marx?"

She shook her head.

"Tell us, Ruth Rose," Dink said.

Ruth Rose pretended to strum a guitar. "I'm Elvis!" she cried.

"That was my next guess," Josh said.

Ruth Rose looked at his mound of green strips. "What are you supposed to be?"

Josh wrapped a strip around his face. He made a swamp monster face at Ruth Rose.

"Guess," he said.

Ruth Rose smiled sweetly. "You're a green sheet torn into strips."

The doorbell rang again.

This time Dink saw a tall man standing on the

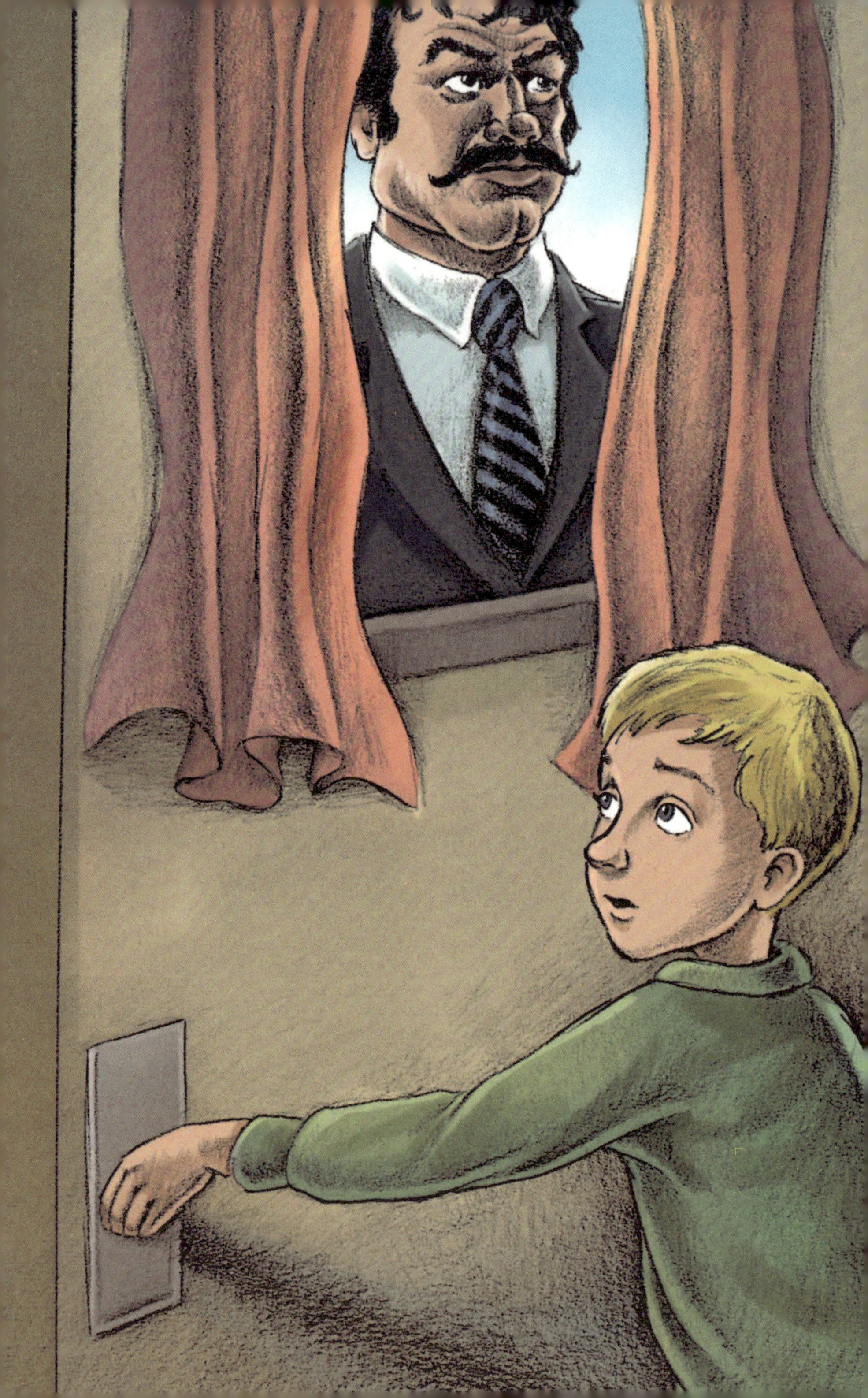

doorstep. He was dressed in a suit and tie. He had dark curly hair, a droopy mustache, and a dimpled chin.

"Hi, there. My name is Detective Reddy. I was hired by the Green Lawn Savings Bank to find someone. Did you hear about the robbery?"

Josh and Ruth Rose came to the door and stood behind Dink.

Dink nodded. "I heard about it on TV."

"Are you looking for the robber?" Josh asked.

Detective Reddy shook his head. "Right now I'm looking for someone who saw him. When the thief ran out of the bank, he took off his mask. Some kid was walking by with a video camera. He got the thief on tape. The bank hired me to find the kid so I can get the video."

"What does the kid look like?" Ruth Rose asked.

Detective Reddy stared at her Elvis wig. "Someone in the bank said he has red hair and he's tall and skinny."

"Sounds like you, Josh," said Dink. He laughed and pointed at Josh's red hair.

"It wasn't me, honest!" Josh said. "I don't even have a video camera."

"No, the kid was a lot older than you," said the detective. "Probably in high school." He patted his mustache. "Do you guys know anyone like that?"

"No," Dink said. "But we do know Green Lawn pretty well. Maybe we can help you find him."

The detective looked at the three friends.

"Tell you what," he said. "Check the high school tomorrow. If you find the kid who filmed the robber, get the video. There'll be a nice reward if you hand it over."

"How much?" Josh asked.

"How about one hundred dollars for each of you?"

"A HUNDRED BUCKS?" screamed Ruth Rose.

Dink, Josh, and Detective Reddy covered their ears.

"Ouch!" said Detective Reddy. "That's quite a set of lungs you've got there."

"How can we get in touch with you if we find the kid?" Dink asked.

The detective pulled out a small pad and a pencil.

He wrote something and ripped off the page.

"Here's my phone number. Call me if you get that video."

Dink closed the door behind Detective Reddy. He grinned at Josh and Ruth Rose. "A hundred bucks each! We're rich!"

Chapter 2

"Here's the plan," Dink said.

It was almost three o'clock the next afternoon. Dink, Josh, and Ruth Rose were headed for the high school, a few blocks away from Green Lawn Elementary.

"Josh, you cover the back door. Ruth Rose, your station is the bike rack. But keep an eye on the parking lot, too."

"How can I watch the bike rack and the parking lot?" asked Ruth Rose.

"Watch one with each eye," Josh said, grinning.

"What's your station?" Ruth Rose asked Dink.

"I'll be watching the front door. If anyone sees a skinny redhead, stop him and yell."

Ruth Rose laughed. "Stop him and yell? He'll think we're crazy and run away."

"She's right," Josh said.

Dink scratched his thick blond hair. "Hmm. Okay, don't yell. Just get his name and tell him he may have won some money."

They cut through the park next to the high school.

"What money?" Josh asked.

"Well, if Detective Reddy is going to pay us a hundred dollars each to find he video, I figure we can give the kid half the money. But only if he gives us the video."

At the high school, they split up. Josh ran around to the back of the school. Ruth Rose sat on the lawn next to the bike rack.

Dink sat on a bench where he had a good view of the front door.

Suddenly, he heard a loud bell. Ten seconds later, the front door burst open. A million high school kids shoved through the door and scrambled down the front steps.

Dink stood on the bench so he wouldn't get trampled. He was looking for red hair, but it wasn't easy to spot. Some of the kids had hats on. Some wore jackets or sweatshirts with the hoods pulled up. Sometimes Dink couldn't tell if a kid was a boy or a girl!

Finally, he spotted a tall guy with red hair. Dink jumped off the bench and ran after him.

"Excuse me," Dink said, trying to catch his breath.

"Who are you?" the redhead asked.

"Dink Duncan." Dink tried to remember his plan. "You may have won some money!"

The redhead stared down at Dink. "Money? Me? Why? How much money?"

"Were you near the bank when the robbery happened last week?" he asked.

The kid kept staring at Dink. "Robbery? What robbery?"

"You didn't hear about it? It was on the news, on TV. Some guy robbed Green Lawn Savings Bank."

"So what's it to you?"

"A kid with red hair got the robber on tape," Dink said. "I'm helping to find him. There's going to be a reward."

"Rats, I wish I did tape the guy," the redhead said, shaking his head. "I could use a reward. But I wasn't anywhere near the bank last week." He waved and headed for the park. "Good luck!"

Dink looked around for another redhead, but everyone had disappeared.

He walked toward the bike rack. Ruth Rose was sitting on the lawn, weaving grass blades together.

"Did you see any redheads?" Dink asked, plopping down beside her.

"Three," Ruth Rose said. "One was a short, fat boy. One was a girl. One was a teacher."

Josh came running up.

"Any luck?" he asked.

"Nope," Dink said. "How'd you do?"

"I talked to two guys with red hair. One of them told me to take a hike. The other one was an exchange student from Ireland. He told me he doesn't even know where the bank is."

"Great," Dink said. "We all struck out. Now what do we do?"

Josh tossed a pine cone at a tree. "Beats me."

"We should search the whole neighborhood," Ruth Rose said.

"How?" Dink asked.

Ruth Rose stood up and dusted off her shorts.

"Easy. We just go door to door and ask."

"How can we do that without our parents finding out?" Josh asked. "Mine won't let me get involved with some bank robber, that's for sure."

"Mine either," Dink said.

"So how do we explain why we're wandering around Green Lawn knocking on everyone's doors?" asked Josh.

"Come on, guys," Ruth Rose said. "Think about it. What's tonight?"

Dink and Josh looked at each other.

"Halloween!"

Chapter 3

With black shoe polish in his hair and plastic fangs in his mouth, Dink looked like Dracula.

His mom had made him a cape from an old black raincoat. He tied the cape around his neck just as the doorbell rang.

A strange creature stood on his porch. The thing was wrapped in green cloth. Tufts of red hair poked out at the top. Large black high-tops stuck out at the bottom.

"How do I look?" the thing asked.

Dink took out his fangs and grinned. "Like some weird vegetable. Half carrot and half asparagus."

Josh shuffled inside the house.

"You look pretty good, Dink. I like the blood dripping down your chin."

The bell dinged again. This time it was a miniature Elvis. Ruth Rose was wearing a white suit with sequins everywhere. She even carried a little guitar. Her Elvis wig made her look about two inches taller.

Ruth Rose strummed her guitar and wiggled her hips.

"Thank you very much, ladies and gentlemen," she said, taking a bow.

"Come on in, Elvis," Dink said. "We have to talk about Operation Redhead before we go trick-or-treating."

They sat at Dink's kitchen table. A basket of candy stood waiting for the neighborhood kids.

"Here's my plan," Dink said. "Every house we go to, we ask if anyone knows a skinny redheaded kid."

"That's my plan!" Ruth Rose said.

Dink grinned. "Oh, yeah, I forgot."

One of Ruth Rose's black eyebrows was crooked.

"We have to keep our eyes peeled. Check out tall kids trick-or-treating."

"Got it," Dink said.

"Anyone with red hair, we ask them if they took a video of the bank robber," Ruth Rose went on.

"Check," Dink said. "Any other ideas?"

"Yeah, I got a great idea," Josh said. "Let's stop talking and get moving!"

Dink's mother walked into the kitchen. She screamed and clutched her chest.

"Oh, my goodness! Monsters in my kitchen!"

Ruth Rose stood up. "I'm not a monster, Mrs. Duncan. I'm Elvis!"

Dink's mom adjusted Ruth Rose's left eyebrow. "I know, honey. You make a great Elvis. But these other two!" She shuddered and made a terrified face.

"We're going now, Mom." Dink fit the plastic fangs over his teeth. He handed Josh a paper bag and took one for himself.

"Please be back in two hours," his mother said.

"Dad and I will have some cider and doughnuts for you."

The three kids each took a different street. They agreed to meet back at Dink's house in about two hours.

Dink headed down Woody Street. He looked at every tall kid in a costume, checking for red hair. But most of the kids out were shorter than him. He counted seventeen ghosts, twenty little witches, eight angels with floppy wings, and a zillion small furry animals.

Dink rang Mrs. Davis's doorbell. "Trick or treat!"

"Oh, hello, Dink!" said Mrs. Davis. She dropped a small bag of candy kisses into his sack.

"Have you seen any redheaded kids tonight?" Dink asked.

"Redheads?" Mrs. Davis patted her white hair. "I'm afraid I don't know anyone besides your friend Josh who has red hair."

Dink thanked Mrs. Davis for the candy and walked next door to old Mr Kramer's house.

Mr. Kramer was a little deaf.

"Do you know a skinny redhead?" asked Dink in a loud voice.

Mr. Kramer turned one ear and leaned toward Dink. "What's that you say? A tinny red bed?"

"A skinny redhead!" Dink yelled even louder. He wished he had Ruth Rose with him. She was the only one loud enough for Mr. Kramer to hear.

Mr. Kramer dropped a nickel in Dink's bag and slammed the door. Dink sighed.

He followed some ghosts to the next house on Woody Street.

A gorilla opened the door when Dink rang the bell. It had a hairy chest and a huge mouth filled with yellow teeth.

"Trick or treat!" said Dink.

The gorilla dropped a banana into Dink's bag.

"Have you seen any tall redheaded teenagers walking around?" Dink asked.

The gorilla grunted and shook his head.

"Thanks anyway," said Dink.

Two hours later, Dink, Josh, and Ruth Rose poured their candy onto Dink's dining room table.

Dink took out his fangs. "Any luck?" he asked.

Josh unwrapped his face. "I saw four redheads. Two girls about ten years old and two adults. No one I talked to knew a skinny redhead in high school."

Ruth Rose took off her wig and eyebrows and dropped them into her plastic jack-o'-lantern.

"Same here," she sighed, slumping in her chair. "Nobody knew the right redhead. And I asked everybody!"

Josh ripped open a miniature bag of M&M's.

"I really wanted that hundred bucks," he said.

光头劫匪

"Maybe we should just forget it."

"Give up after just two days? Noway, you guys!" Dink climbed up on the table. He wrapped his cape around his face so just his eyes showed.

In his best Count Dracula voice, he said, "Vee vill never giff up!"

Chapter 4

The next morning, Dink's hair was stiff with black shoe polish. He shampooed three times before he got out of the shower.

The bathroom mirror was fogged up when he tried to see his reflection. He wiped the mirror, looked at himself, and gasped.

His hair wasn't its usual blond and it wasn't vampire black. It was a muddy brown color, like the rusty parts on his bike.

"Mom! Help!"

His mother peeked into the bathroom. "What's the…oh, I see." She giggled.

光头劫匪

"It's not funny, Mom. How am I supposed to go outside like this? My hair looks like it rusted!"

"Honey, lots of kids will have traces of makeup on their faces or color in their hair today. It's the day after Halloween."

Dink rubbed a towel over his hair as hard as he could. He looked in the mirror. Now he had frizzy rust-colored hair.

"Be thankful it's Saturday," his mother said, smiling. "At least you don't have to go to school today."

After breakfast, Dink jammed his baseball cap over his hair and headed for Josh's house.

When Dink got there, Josh was already shooting hoops in front of his barn. He grinned at Dink.

"What's wrong with your hair?" he asked.

Dink yanked his hat off. "Take a look. The stupid shoe polish from last night won't wash out. I had to be a vampire, right? I couldn't just be a cowboy or an astronaut."

Josh dribbled and took a shot. He missed the hoop.

"So have you thought of a plan for finding that kid with the video?" Josh asked.

"No," said Dink, jamming his hat back over his hair.

"Well, what do we do now?" said Josh. "Ask at more houses?"

"I don't know," Dink said. "Now that Halloween is over, we'd look pretty suspicious. Besides, Green Lawn has hundreds of houses. We'd be knocking on doors for a month."

Josh made a perfect shot. "Two points!"

"We have to use our heads instead of our feet," Dink said, grabbing the ball after Josh's basket.

A door slammed behind them.

"Uh-oh," Josh mumbled.

"Josh, it's time to go," his mother called. "Come in and brush your teeth, please."

"I have a dentist appointment," Josh said. "Call me later, okay?"

"Okay." Dink tossed Josh's ball into the barn and started walking away.

"Hey!" Josh yelled behind him. "I think your new

hair color looks just adorable!"

"Very funny," Dink muttered, tugging his hat down even tighter.

Maybe I'll cut my hair off, he thought. Go to school bald on Monday.

Suddenly, he stopped walking. Thinking about cutting his hair off gave him an idea.

He ran toward Main Street. At Howard's Barbershop, he peered through the glass. Howard was watching an *I Love Lucy* rerun on a small TV set.

Dink walked in, setting off the sleigh bells hanging over the door. Whenever he came to Howard's for a haircut, Dink thought about Christmas.

"What'll it be today, Dink?" Howard asked. "Want a flattop? How about one of them Mohawk jobbies, with the stripe down the middle?"

"I don't want a haircut," Dink said. "I need to ask you something."

Howard squinted one blue eye. He lifted Dink's baseball cap. "What happened to your hair?"

Dink blushed. "I was a vampire last night. I used black shoe polish in my hair and it won't come out. I tried."

Howard grinned. "Hop up in the chair, me lad. I'll dose you with me special shampoo. You can ask your question while I perform a little magic."

Dink hung his hat on a peg and climbed into the barber chair. Howard pulled a bottle and some white towels out of a cupboard.

"I was wondering if you know any kids with red hair," Dink said. "Besides Josh."

Howard draped a towel around Dink's shoulders and pinned it in back. He misted Dink's hair with a spray bottle of water.

"I might," he answered. "Why, do you want me to dye your hair red?"

Dink laughed. "No, I'm looking for a certain kid who has red hair. I think he's a teenager."

"I know one teenager who had red hair," Howard said, pouring green shampoo onto Dink's hair. "But I shaved it all off last week. Came running in here all excited, out of breath. 'Shave my head!' he tells me. So I did."

The smell of the shampoo made Dink's eyes water. He felt his heart start to tap-dance.

"Was he carrying a video camera?" Dink asked.

Howard rubbed the shampoo into Dink's hair.

"Why all the questions about this redheaded boy?" he asked.

Dink thought for a few seconds, then decided to spill the beans. He told Howard about the bank robber, about the kid with the video camera, and about the three hundred dollars the detective had promised.

Howard chuckled. "Oh, now I see why the boy ran in here yelling for me to cut off all his hair. He didn't want the bank bandit to recognize him. So if I tell you this lad's name, you're going to persuade him to give you the videotape?"

"Yes, if I can," Dink said.

"What about the money?" said Howard.

Dink looked at Howard in the mirror. "What about it?"

"Would you be planning to share the reward with the redheaded boy?"

Dink grinned. "Sure. We'll give him half of what we get from the detective."

"That sounds like a fine idea." Howard rubbed Dink's hair vigorously. Dink watched in the mirror. His hair was a slimy green mess.

"Does this stuff really get shoe polish out?" he asked.

"Yup. Invented it meself," Howard said. "Secret recipe. I used it once to get bubble gum out of me granddaughter's hair. It took tar out of our dog's fur, too."

Howard swung the barber chair around and lowered its back. He positioned Dink's head over the sink.

"Close your eyes, me boy. Let's wash this gook out and see what's what."

Dink liked the feel of the warm water and Howard's fingers smoothing the shampoo out of his hair. After a few minutes, Howard sat him up and plopped a fresh towel on his head.

"Dry off. I think you're back to normal."

Dink rubbed his hair with the towel, then looked in the mirror. He laughed out loud. "You did it!"

Howard smiled at Dink's reflection. "I should sell this stuff and make a million dollars."

"How much do I owe you?" Dink asked.

"This one's on me, young fella. And the boy with red hair is Lucky O'Leary. He lives over on Robin Road with his mum and his little brothers and sisters. All six of 'em! Nice kids, and every last one's a redhead."

Howard grinned as he lowered the chair. "Except for Lucky, who suddenly decided to go bald."

Chapter 5

"He's bald?" Josh said, climbing Ruth Rose's front steps.

Dink had run right home from the barbershop and called Josh. Now they were picking up Ruth Rose so they could go to Robin Road together.

"That's what Howard said," Dink told Josh. He pushed the doorbell.

"So that's why we didn't spot him at the high school!" Josh said.

"COME IN!" Ruth Rose screamed from inside.

Ruth Rose was sitting on the floor watching a video with her four-year-old brother, Nate.

"Come on, Ruth Rose. I think we found the redhead!" Dink said. "We're going to his house."

Ruth Rose jumped up and screamed, "I'M LEAVING WITH THE GUYS, MOM! WATCH NATE!"

Dink and Josh covered their ears.

Ruth Rose told Nate, "You stay right here and wait for Mommy, okay?"

Nate nodded and kept his eyes on the TV set.

"Let's go." Ruth Rose led the way back to the door and skipped down the front steps.

"How'd you find the kid?" she asked.

Dink explained how he hadn't been able to get the shoe polish out of his hair.

"That made me think about cutting my hair off. And that made me think about the barbershop. Who would know all the redheads in Green Lawn?"

"HOWARD THE BARBER!" she screamed.

The boys covered their ears again.

"I'm going to need a hearing aid like old Mr. Kramer," Josh muttered.

Dink had looked up O'Leary in the phone book to

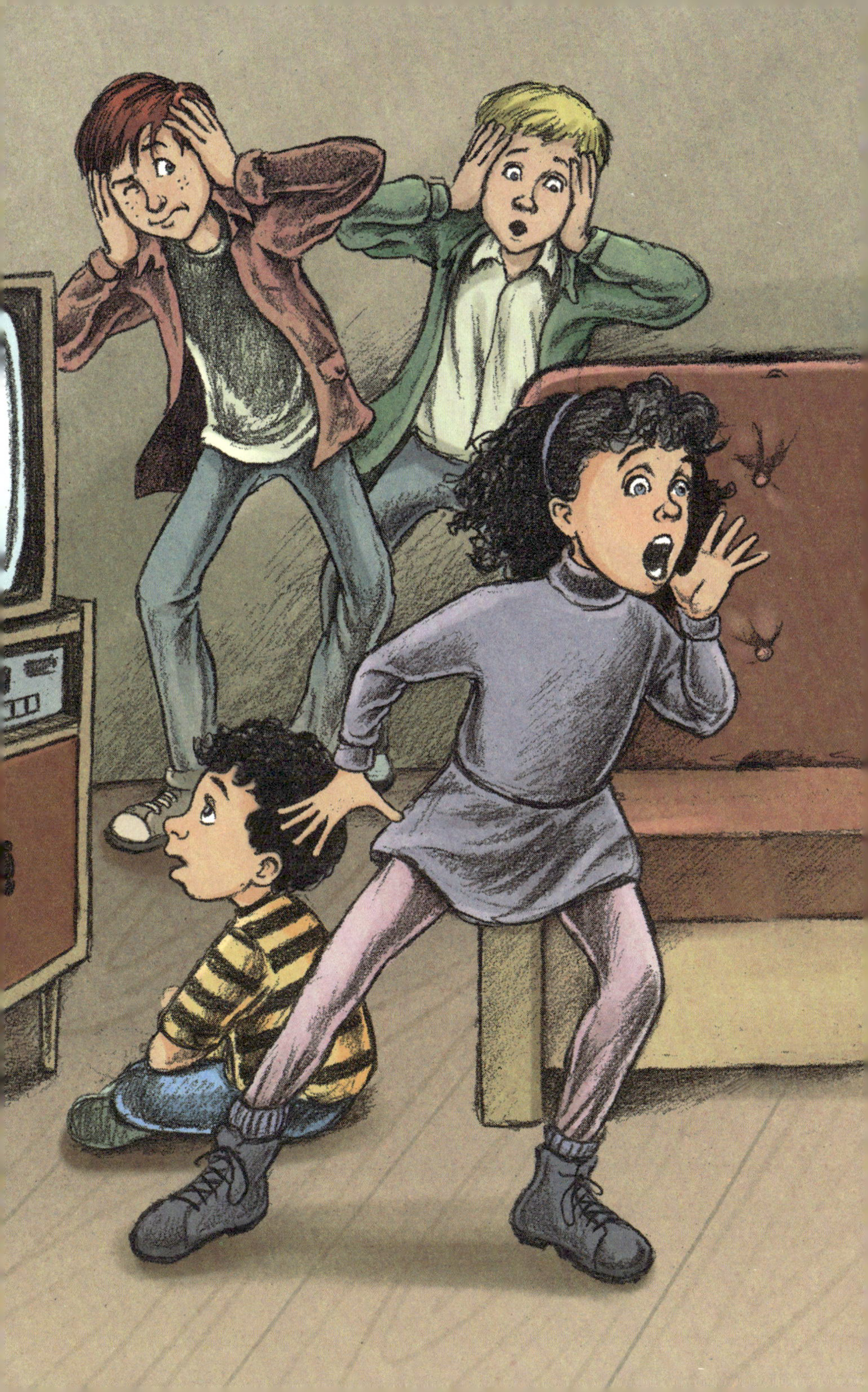

get the address on Robin Road. They stopped in front of house number 33. It was a big blue house with toys and bikes and sneakers and basketballs all over the lawn. Loud music came out through the front door.

They walked onto the porch and stepped over a baseball bat. Four pumpkins sat in a row, all carved with scary faces.

Dink rang the bell. "Keep your fingers crossed," he said.

A little girl opened the door. She had red hair and a face full of freckles.

"Hi! I'm Josephine and I'm five and a half!" She held up ten fingers.

"Is your brother home?" Dink asked.

"Which one? I have this many!" Josephine held up ten fingers again.

Dink laughed. "Do you have a big brother named Lucky?"

The music went off.

"Who's out there, Jo?" a voice called. A tall, skinny teenager wearing torn jeans and a T-shirt came up behind Josephine. Dink noticed red fuzz covering his

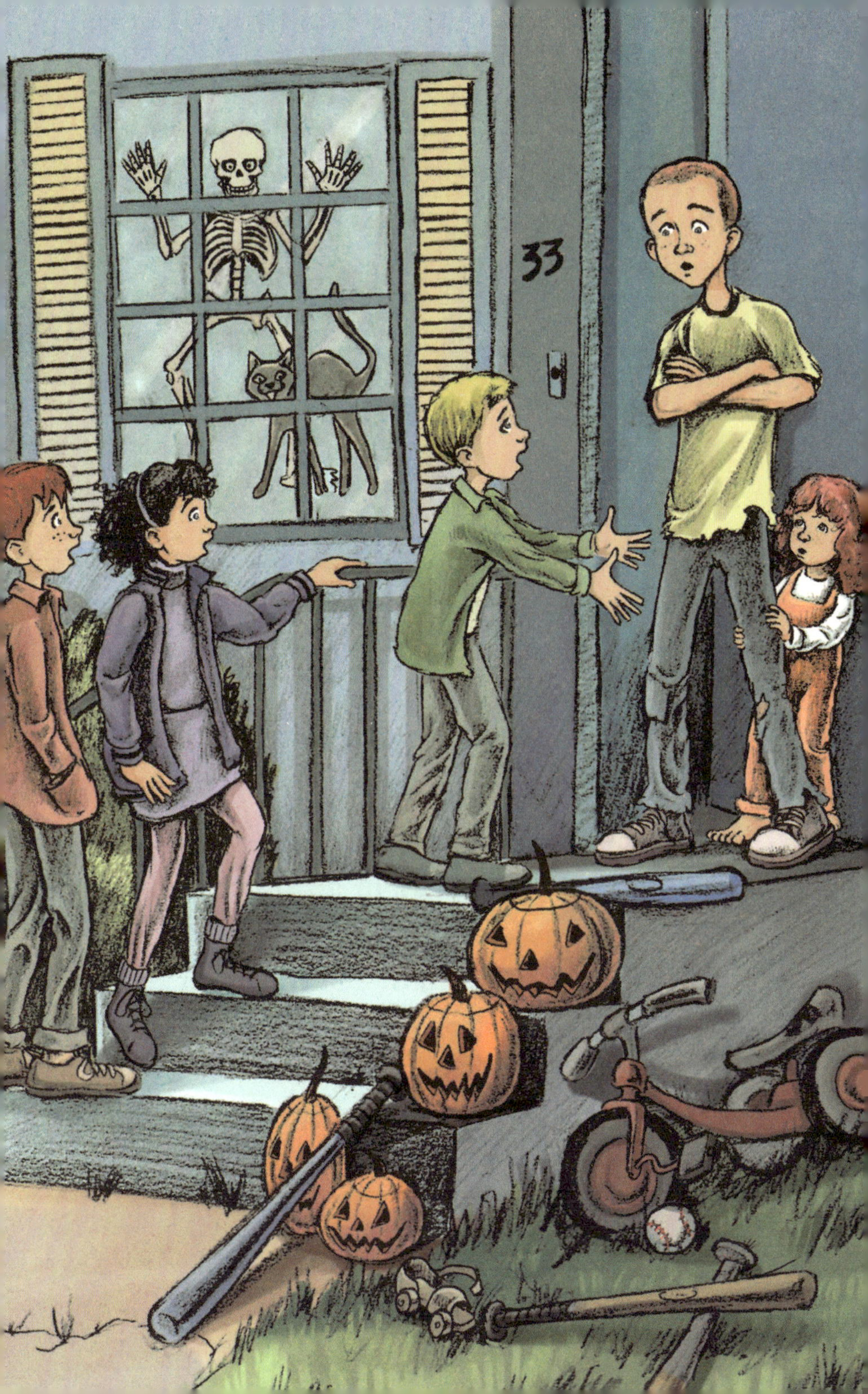
33

head, like a new red lawn.

"Are you Lucky O'Leary?" Dink asked.

The kid looked down at Dink and Josh and Ruth Rose. "Who wants to know?"

"We do," Ruth Rose said. "How'd you like to earn some money?"

"I might," he said.

"We're looking for a kid who got the Green Lawn bank robber on video last week," Dink said. "The bank hired a detective to find the video, and we're helping the detective. He's paying us to get the video, and we'll split the money with you. If you're the kid, I mean."

"Are you?" Ruth Rose asked.

The kid rubbed the top of his fuzzy red head. "Yeah," he muttered. "I'm the guy."

Then he crossed his arms. "But I'm not giving my tape to any detective."

Chapter 6

The kids stared at Lucky.

"Why not?" Ruth Rose asked. "The detective is helping the bank find the robber. You could be a HERO!"

"Shh!" said Lucky. He looked around nervously. Then he beckoned Dink, Josh, and Ruth Rose inside.

"Come on."

Inside Lucky's house, the kids followed him down a hallway into his bedroom. Dink noticed that he was limping. His room had posters of basketball players on the walls. There were clothes all over the floor.

Lucky flopped down on his bed.

"Listen," he said. "I'm afraid to give that tape to the detective. What if the robber found out I handed it over? With my luck, he'd come after me."

"How would the robber know it was you who taped him?" Dink asked.

Lucky sat up. "Because he looked right at me when he ran out of the bank. The guy saw me taping him! That's why I ran to Howard's to get my head shaved." Lucky scratched his fuzzy head.

"But if you turn in the tape, the robber will get caught. Then you won't have to worry about him at all," said Josh.

"Besides, we'll give you half of our reward," Ruth Rose said. "Right, guys?"

"Right," Dink said. "Is Lucky your real name?"

The kid shook his head. "It's Paul. Lucky is my nickname. People call me that because I always have such rotten luck. Since school started, my dog died, my bike got stolen, and I broke my toe. I can barely walk to school."

"You can buy a new bike with the reward money," Ruth Rose said. "Then you won't have to walk."

Lucky smiled at Ruth Rose. "I'm saving all my money for college," he said. Then he sighed. "It seems like I'll never get enough."

Lucky thought for a minute.

"Listen, that reward money would really help," he said. "But you guys have to promise not to tell who gave you the video."

They all nodded.

"Okay," said Lucky. He got off the bed and limped over to his closet. He pulled a box from the top shelf. The box was filled with videotapes. He handed one of the tapes to Dink.

Lucky looked embarrassed. "Um… when can I get the money?" he asked.

"Maybe tomorrow," Dink said. "We'll let you know, okay?"

"Sure, that'll be fine," said Lucky. He pretended to zip his lips closed. "And remember, you promised not to tell anyone where you got the video. Not even that detective."

The kids nodded again.

Lucky walked them to the door, stepping around

a pile of kids wrestling on the living room floor. Dink noticed they all had red hair and freckles.

Josephine popped up out of the pile.

"Bye!" she said, smiling at Dink.

光头劫匪

As soon as they were on the sidewalk, Dink, Josh, and Ruth Rose triple-high-fived each other.

"We got it!" Josh yelled.

Dink slipped the tape into his pocket. "Now we just have to call Detective Reddy and get our money!"

Chapter 7

The kids hurried back to Dink's house. There was no one home. Dink opened the front door with his key.

He saw a note on the kitchen table.

DAD AND I ARE OUT SHOPPING.
WE'LL BE BACK SOON.
HAVE A SNACK.
LOVE, MOM

Dink was glad his folks were out. He knew they wouldn't like him playing detective. When this was all over, he'd tell them how he earned the hundred bucks.

Josh opened Dink's refrigerator. "What do you have to eat?" he asked.

Dink set the tape on the counter. "There should be some doughnuts on the counter."

He pulled the paper with the detective's number on it out of his pocket. He called the number.

"Hello, is this Detective Reddy? This is Dink Duncan. Me and my friends found that video for you. What? No, we haven't looked at it. Okay. Bye."

Dink hung up smiling. "He'll be right over. He said we were good detectives. He told us not to look at the video."

Josh was eating a doughnut. "Why not?" he said with his mouth full.

"He said it was top secret."

They all looked at each other.

"Come on!" Dink said, grabbing the video.

They ran into the living room. Dink turned on the TV and slid the tape into the VCR.

The first part of the video showed a big dog chewing on a rubber bone. Then they saw a girl in a bathing suit. She was laughing and running away from the camera. Next came a birthday party. Most of the people in the picture looked like Lucky O'Leary. Dink recognized little Josephine.

Finally, they saw the front of the Green Lawn Savings Bank. The door opened and a man came running out. He was pulling off a ski mask.

"That must be the robber!" Dink said. He pressed

the pause button.

The man on the tape was completely bald. His head was shiny in the sunlight. He was wearing sweatpants and a sweatshirt, and he was carrying a gym bag. He had a surprised look on his face.

"That must be when he noticed Lucky taping him," Josh said.

Ruth Rose moved closer to the TV. "Look, he's got a dimple on his chin."

Suddenly, Ruth Rose gasped. She ran across

the room and out of the house. The door slammed behind her.

Dink looked at Josh. "What's going on?"

Josh shrugged. "Maybe she doesn't like guys with dimples."

A minute later, the door burst open and Ruth Rose ran back in. She was carrying her Elvis wig and her fake eyebrows.

Ruth Rose stuck one eyebrow on the TV screen, under the bandit's nose. It looked like a mustache. She held the wig over the bandit's bald head.

"Who does that look like?" she demanded.

Josh jumped into the air. "Oh, my gosh! The bank robber looks exactly like Detective Reddy!"

Just then the doorbell rang. Dink peeked through the front window.

"Who is it?" Josh asked.

Dink's eyes were bugging out when he turned around. "It's Detective Reddy!"

Chapter 8

Ruth Rose snatched the wig and eyebrow off the TV and hid them behind her back.

Josh pushed the eject button and slid the video inside his shirt.

Dink stared at the door. He didn't think he could walk.

The bell rang again.

Dink looked at his friends. Then he took a deep breath and opened the door.

Ruth Rose slipped out just as Detective Reddy walked in.

"Hi, there," said Detective Reddy. He grinned at

Dink and Josh. "Gee, you kids are clever. How'd you find the redhead with the video?"

Dink stared at the man in front of him. He couldn't believe it. Detective Reddy wasn't a detective at all. He was a bank robber! And he was standing in Dink's own living room!

"We were just lucky, I guess," Dink mumbled.

The man patted his mustache. "So where is it?"

Dink wouldn't let his eyes look at the lump under Josh's shirt. "Where's what?"

"The video. You called and said you had the video. So where is it?"

Dink's mind went blank. He didn't know what to say.

Think, Dink! he commanded himself.

Josh came to the rescue. "We hid the tape upstairs, remember, Dink?"

Dink stared at Josh. "Huh? Oh, yeah, now I remember." He grinned at the man. "We wanted to make sure no one saw it before we gave it to you."

"Come on, Dink." Josh headed for the stairs.

"It takes two of you to get one video?" the man

said.

"Well...um...it's in my mother's room." Dink held up his front door key. "I'm the only one allowed to unlock her door."

Dink hurried up the stairs behind Josh. They ran into Dink's bedroom and shut the door.

Dink's guinea pig, Loretta, started squeaking and running around in her cage.

"Not now, Loretta," Dink said.

"Where'd Ruth Rose go?" said Josh. "I can't believe she ditched us!"

Dink didn't answer. He paced back and forth in front of his bed. He tugged on his hair. He snapped his fingers nervously.

"Dink, stop, I'm getting dizzy," Josh said. "What're we gonna do?"

Dink stopped. "I don't know! We can't give him the video. He'll destroy it. Then nobody can prove anything! He'll get away scot-free. And he might even go after Lucky!"

"We have to catch him and hand him over to the cops," Josh said. "Do you have any rope? We'll jump him and tie him up!"

"I don't keep rope in my bedroom, Josh," Dink said. "Besides, he's bigger and stronger than us. He might even have a gun!"

"Need any help up there?" the man yelled.

Dink opened his door a crack. "No thanks. We'll

be right down."

Dink grabbed a soccer video from his bookshelf and handed it to Josh.

"Let's give him this."

"But what happens when he finds out it's not the real video?" Josh asked.

"I don't know. But we don't have any choice."

Josh pulled Lucky's video out of his shirt. He dropped it in Loretta's cage and covered it with shavings.

"Guard it, Loretta," he said.

They walked downstairs. Dink tried to smile.

"We found it!" he said.

Josh handed over the soccer video.

Just then the front door flew open. Ruth Rose was standing there with Officer Fallon and Officer Keene from the Green Lawn Police Department.

Dink was never so happy to see anyone.

"That's him!" Ruth Rose declared. She pointed at the man holding the video tape. "He robbed the Green Lawn bank!"

The officers stepped into the living room.

The man smiled. "I'm a private detective, officers," he said.

"Mind showing us some identification, sir?" said Officer Fallon.

The man patted his mustache. "I don't have my wallet with me."

"You don't?" Officer Keene said. "Detectives are required to carry their identification at all times."

"Sure, and normally I do. But I left my wallet in the car. I'll get it and be right back."

"His mustache is fake!" Ruth Rose said, stepping in front of the officers. "And so is that wig!"

Everybody stared at the man.

Suddenly, he grabbed Ruth Rose and held her in front of him.

"Outta my way!" he yelled. "I'm leaving, and the girl's coming with me!"

Ruth Rose took a deep breath.

Then she let out the loudest scream of her life.

"AIIIIIIIIIEEEEEEEE!"

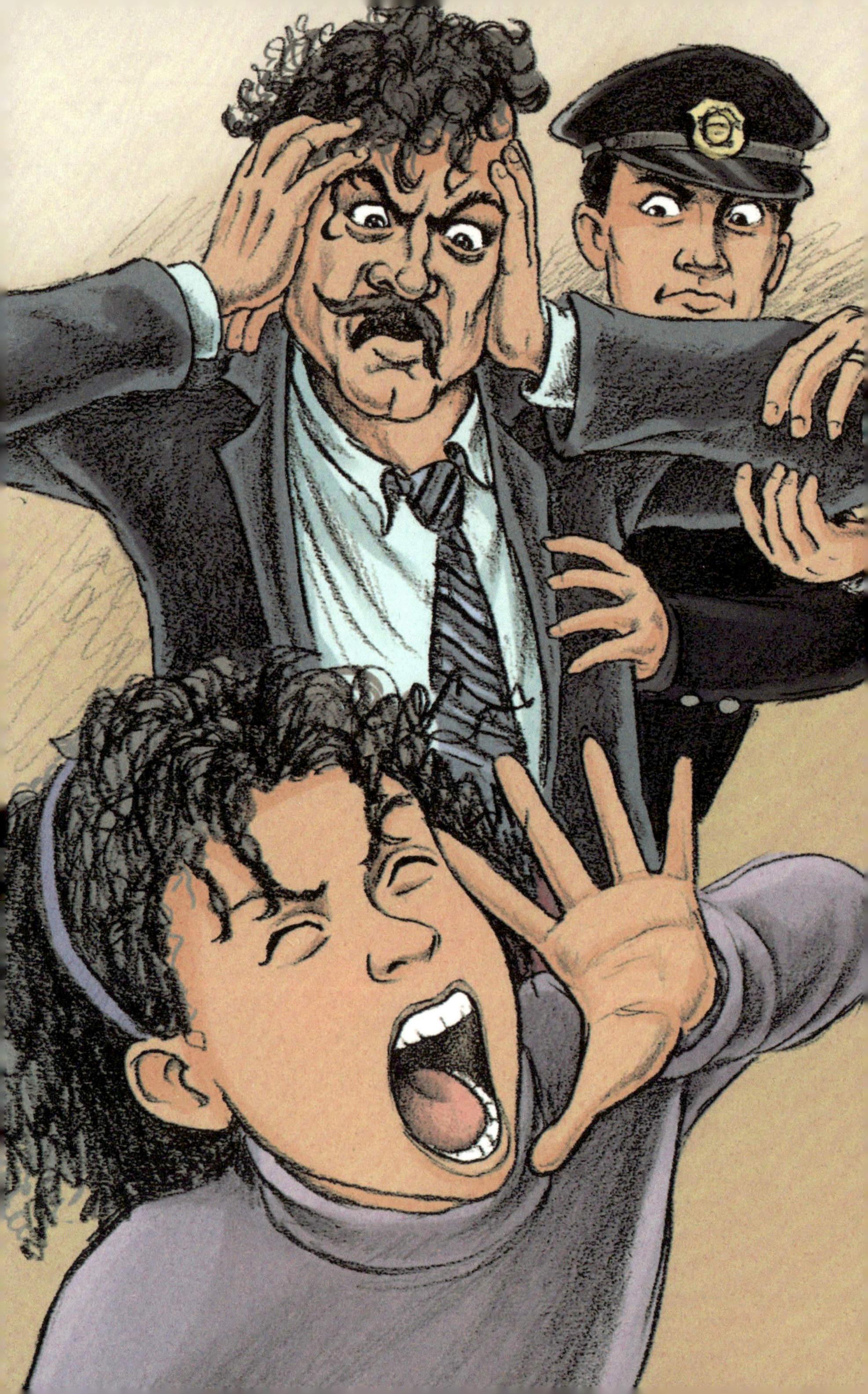

Chapter 9

Josh, Dink, and the officers covered their ears.

"Ouch!" cried the bank robber.

He stumbled backward, clapping his hands over his ears.

The minute he let go of Ruth Rose, Officer Fallon grabbed him.

"It's all over, fella," Officer Fallon said. He snapped handcuffs on the man's wrists.

Officer Keene pulled off the thief's fake mustache

and wig. Now the man looked just the way he did in the video. He had a shiny bald head and a surprised look on his face.

Officer Keene took him outside.

Officer Fallon put his hand on Ruth Rose's shoulder. "Ruth Rose, are you all right?"

Ruth Rose nodded. "I'm fine, Officer Fallon."

"So where's this videotape you told me about?"

Josh ran upstairs and got Lucky's video. He came back and slid it into the VCR. While they watched, Dink told Officer Fallon how it all happened.

Officer Fallon laughed. "Pretty clever of our thief. He hired you to find the video with his own face in it. If he got rid of the tape, no one could prove he was in that bank."

"He couldn't look for the tape himself," Ruth Rose explained. "The kid who taped him might have recognized him, like I did."

"How did you kids get hold of this video?" Officer Fallon asked.

Dink remembered their promise to Lucky. "We can't tell where we got it. We promised."

Officer Fallon smiled. "Well, whoever caught that guy on tape deserves a reward. Speaking of which, I believe you kids will be sharing a five-thousand-dollar reward from the bank."

"Five thousand dollars!" Josh jumped out of his seat. He and Dink did a little dance around the living room.

Officer Fallon laughed. "Ruth Rose here is a brave girl. She snuck over to her house and called the police station."

Ruth Rose turned her favorite shade of pink.

When Officer Fallon left, Ruth Rose did some math on Dink's calculator. "After we give Lucky his half, we'll each get $833. 33," she said. "With a penny left over."

"We're rich!" said Josh. "Let's spend it!"

Dink laughed. "Mine's going into my savings account."

"Mine, too," Ruth Rose said. "I'm saving for a computer."

Josh slumped into a chair. "Yeah, you're right. My folks would kill me if I blew eight hundred bucks on

131

pizza and ice cream."

On Monday, Dink, Josh, and Ruth Rose ran to the high school as soon as Green Lawn Elementary let out. They sat on a bench in front of the high school, out of breath.

"What did Lucky say when you told him he's getting half of five thousand dollars?" Josh asked.

"Nothing," Dink said, smiling. "I didn't tell him."

Just then the bell rang. A few seconds later, kids came streaming out of the high school.

"There he is!" Ruth Rose ran to meet Lucky O'Leary. She brought him over to the bench. He was smiling.

"Ruth Rose says you got paid. Did you bring my hundred and fifty?" he asked.

Dink shook his head sadly. "Not exactly."

"What do you mean, 'Not exactly'?"

The three friends burst out laughing.

"We don't have a hundred and fifty dollars, but we do have this," said Dink.

He handed Lucky a check for $2,500.

Lucky's mouth and eyes popped open. "Twenty-five hundred bucks!" he yelled. "Where did this come from?"

"That's your half of the reward from the bank," Dink said. "We looked at your tape when we got home. Ruth Rose recognized the robber. He turned out to be the detective, only he wasn't really a detective. He was just pretending to be one so he could find you to get your video."

Lucky blinked. "So you guys nabbed him?"

"Yeah, right in Dink's house!" Josh said. "Ruth Rose snuck out and called the cops."

"It was exciting!" said Ruth Rose.

Lucky stared at his check again. He shook his head and grinned. "This is my lucky day. Now my mom can get the kids all their school stuff and have the car fixed."

"What about college?" Dink asked. "I thought that's what you were going to do with your money."

Lucky shook his head. "College is out for now. I'll have to work for awhile till Mom and I can save more." Lucky looked at his check. "Maybe next year."

He shook hands with the three kids. "Anyway, thanks a lot for this check. I can't wait to see my mom's face when I give it to her!"

Dink watched Lucky walk away. Only he wasn't limping as much today.

"I wonder how many college courses Lucky could buy with my $833. 33," he said.

Ruth Rose smiled at Dink. "I wonder how many college books he could buy with mine," she said.

Josh stared. "What? You're giving your money to Lucky? But you earned it!"

Dink shook his head. "No, we didn't. We just ran around talking to people. Lucky really earned the reward money."

"That's right," Ruth Rose said. "He's the one who caught the robber on videotape."

Dink and Ruth Rose started walking toward Main Street.

"Hey, where you guys going?" Josh yelled.

"To the bank," Dink said over his shoulder. "And then to Lucky's house."

Ruth Rose turned around and looked at Josh. "You

光头劫匪

coming with us?"

Josh grinned, then caught up with Dink and Ruth Rose. "I wonder how many college meals Lucky can buy with my $833. 33," he said.

"Race you to the bank!" said Ruth Rose.

And the three friends took off.

Text copyright © 1997 by Ron Roy
Cover art copyright © 2015 by Stephen Gilpin
Interior illustrations copyright © 1997 by John Steven Gurney
All rights reserved. Published in the United States by Random House Children's Books,
a division of Random House LLC, a Penguin Random House Company, New York.
Originally published in paperback by Random House Children's Books, New York, in 1997.

本书中英双语版由中南博集天卷文化传媒有限公司与企鹅兰登（北京）文化发展有限公司合作出版。

"企鹅"及其相关标识是企鹅兰登已经注册或尚未注册的商标。
未经允许，不得擅用。
封底凡无企鹅防伪标识者均属未经授权之非法版本。

©中南博集天卷文化传媒有限公司。本书版权受法律保护。未经权利人许可，任何人不得以任何方式使用本书包括正文、插图、封面、版式等任何部分内容，违者将受到法律制裁。

著作权合同登记号：字18-2023-258

图书在版编目（CIP）数据

光头劫匪 ：汉英对照／（美）罗恩·罗伊著 ；（美）约翰·史蒂文·格尼绘 ；曹幼南译. -- 长沙 ：湖南少年儿童出版社，2024.10. -- （A to Z神秘案件）.
ISBN 978-7-5562-7817-6
Ⅰ．H319.4
中国国家版本馆CIP数据核字第2024LU6094号

A TO Z SHENMI ANJIAN GUANGTOU JIEFEI
A to Z神秘案件 光头劫匪
［美］罗恩·罗伊 著　［美］约翰·史蒂文·格尼 绘　曹幼南 译

责任编辑：唐凌 李炜	策划出品：李炜 张苗苗 文赛峰
策划编辑：文赛峰	特约编辑：张晓璐
营销编辑：付佳 杨朔 周晓茜	封面设计：霍雨佳
版权支持：王媛媛	版式设计：马睿君
插图上色：河北传图文化	内文排版：马睿君

出 版 人：刘星保
出　　版：湖南少年儿童出版社
地　　址：湖南省长沙市晚报大道89号
邮　　编：410016
电　　话：0731-82196320
常年法律顾问：湖南崇民律师事务所　柳成柱律师
经　　销：新华书店

开　本：875 mm×1230 mm　1/32	印　刷：三河市中晟雅豪印务有限公司
字　数：74千字	印　张：4.25
版　次：2024年10月第1版	印　次：2024年10月第1次印刷
书　号：ISBN 978-7-5562-7817-6	定　价：280.00元（全10册）

若有质量问题，请致电质量监督电话：010-59096394　团购电话：010-59320018